RAISING TO THE CHALLENGE

A FUNDRAISING FABLE

SCHUYLER LEHMAN

FOREWORD BY DR. LARRY TAYLOR

Copyright ©2020 Schuyler D. Lehman, Sr.

All rights reserved. No part of this book may be reproduced in any form without written permission from author.

This is a work of fiction. Names, characters, places, and incidents either are the products of the author's imagination or are used fictitiously. Any resemblance to actual persons, living or dead, businesses, companies, or events is entirely coincidental.

ISBN-13: 979-8645124168

Table of Contents

Foreword	5
Introduction	9
Part I	11
Part II	35
Part III	73
Part IV	117
Part V	143
Conclusion	171
Key Concepts	175

Raising to the Challenge

Foreword by Dr. Larry Taylor

I first met Schuyler Lehman in 2014 during my tenure as Head of School at Prestonwood Christian Academy (PCA) in Plano, Texas. I had heard through a couple of reliable references that he had some fresh ideas for fundraising that supported a Christian school model. We invited Schuyler to come and address our board during our annual retreat with an eye toward inspiring our trustees to engage in our funding model in new and creative ways.

I have been around long enough to see through most of the fog that consultants can sometimes create about so-called new approaches. And I had used consultants on several previous occasions to help our school through the capital campaign process. But the message that Schuyler shared with our trustees that late summer day in 2014 was simple and it stuck.

For years, fundraising has been thought to be something along the lines of "a necessary evil" to make the budget balance in our growing efforts to provide the best quality Christ-centered education possible. And while we had received many extremely generous gifts from Godly believers in our mission, we had never taken seriously one key concept – that we had a second mission to serve the needs of those who have the means to fund our primary mission.

Over the next year our trustees and I concluded that PCA would launch a capital campaign to build a new middle school and fine arts facility. So, we set about the task of selecting a consultant to help us with the due diligence step of conducting a feasibility study. We looked at a few firms, one of which was Schuyler's firm (Mission Advancement Professionals), and quickly concluded that Schuyler's philosophy and approach was right for the culture of PCA. Fast forward a few years – that decision proved to be an important one for PCA.

Most of our previous campaign efforts had yielded modest results of four to six million dollars to help us tackle buildings one at a time. The campaign through which the MAP team guided us was aimed at raising nearly five times that amount. The feasibility study was conducted in such a way that the foundation for success was poured before the campaign began. And three years later, we were cutting the ribbon for our new middle school and fine arts facility.

Let me back up a few steps – I am not writing this forward to simply recommend a good consultant. I have come to believe in the philosophical approach to fundraising to which Schuyler has dedicated his life. And it truly is unique and different from others in the consulting field. In our work with Schuyler, we approached people from a completely new perspective, with prayer, patience, and discipline. The result was that we received the largest gifts we have ever received by a long shot.

The book you are about to read is one that lays out the essence of this philosophy and approach. Schuyler does this in the form of a fable with characters to whom readers will relate. I believe that there are many Christian schools and nonprofits alike that will benefit from this read. I hope and pray that you have the same experience as PCA did by exploring deeper Schuyler's approach to funding the ministry of Christian education.

Dr. Larry Taylor is the president and CEO of The Association of Christian Schools International (ACSI), an organization that serves to strengthen Christian schools and equip Christian educators worldwide as they prepare students academically and inspire them to become devoted followers of Jesus Christ. He previously served 19 years as head of school at Prestonwood Christian Academy in Plano, Texas.

Raising to the Challenge

Introduction

After reading countless development books and writing two of my own, I took some time off from writing to ponder how the message of my firm (Mission Advancement Professionals) could be delivered more effectively. Our goal is to be a resource to the nonprofit world and specifically, as my friends and clients know well, faith-based schools and human service agencies.

We have tried many different formats for delivering our counsel, from webinars, training videos, workshops, podcasts, even two books titled *The Perfect Campaign* and *The Perfect Development Office*, and all mediums are effective to an extent. But the question remains, how can we share our knowledge and experience in a format that fits a real-life scenario?

This book is my attempt to answer that question. I have taken several key Mission Advancement Professionals (MAP) principles that make up our philosophical approach to relationship-based fundraising and applied them to a fictional nonprofit organization that has leaders who are just as wonderful (and quirky) as we encounter in our daily lives.

In addition, this is my first attempt at writing fiction, and I will be the first to acknowledge how very different this kind of writing is. Nevertheless, it was great fun to create, and it delivers the MAP message in a creative way. At the end of the book, you'll find a summary of Key Concepts and suggestions for applying them to your own nonprofit organization.

While the story unfolds in places where I have spent much time and that are familiar to me, all characters and nonprofit organizations in this book are fictitious and not intended to resemble any people I know or organizations with which I am familiar. I have taken a few attributes from friends and colleagues I have known over the years and combined them into the main characters. But any other similarities to real people is purely coincidental.

I hope you enjoy this story.

PART I

In a clock, stop but one wheel and you stop every wheel, because they are dependent upon one other. So when God has ordered a thing for the present to be thus and thus, how do you know how many things depend upon this thing? God may have some work to do twenty years hence that depends on this passage of providence that falls out this day or this week.

— Jeremiah Burroughs, <u>The Rare Jewel of Christian Contentment</u>

July 2, 4:48 a.m., Red River, New Mexico

Alan Morgan awoke extra early after a restless and practically sleepless night. He thought in frustration, *This is supposed to be my vacation for crying out loud—my time to relax and unplug. A little rest is all I ask.*

He knew what it was: financial worries—or *crisis* to be more accurate. Not for him personally, but for Lakeview Christian Academy, the school where Alan served as headmaster in McKinney, Texas, a suburb of Dallas.

Alan and his wife, Carol, who teaches social studies at Lakeview Christian, had just arrived the previous day in Red River, New Mexico, for their summer vacation. The two lifelong educators, along with their two children, Tyler and Amy, had been coming to Red River every year since the kids were tiny. With both kids now in college and using the summer months to get ahead on studies, this was the first year for Alan and Carol to make the trip without either of them.

Alan had wondered whether he and Carol should have even made the trip this year. After all, so many of their experiences in the sleepy mountain town revolved around the kids. In the end, Carol convinced Alan that the trip would be good for both of them to relax and get away from the stress of Lakeview Christian. And given the tone of the school's last board meeting, Alan agreed that some time away in the mountains to reflect and problem solve would probably be a good thing.

The clock on the nightstand read 4:48 a.m. in red digital numbers. Although the bedroom window showed the sky was still dark, he knew that he would not be able to go back to sleep at this point.

And it would be a good four hours before Carol would wake up. So, he decided to get up and start a pot of coffee.

With a warm mug in hand and seated in his favorite spot on the couch, he had to admit that being up at this early hour was incredibly peaceful. As he gazed out the large picture window from his comfortable seat in the family room, there was just a hint of light to give the scenery a blue hue. The forest was just visible beyond the pond in front of their place. A family of deer was foraging about at the edge of the trees completely unaware of any humans who might be watching.

Red River is located in the northern New Mexico Rocky Mountains, just south of the Colorado border. Perched in a valley at an altitude of over 8,000 feet, Red River is a ski resort in the winter. But in the summer, Red River is a retreat for families mostly from Texas and Oklahoma wishing to escape the blazing heat of the south. The mountains afford spectacular views, hiking, and other family recreation.

Alan sat and daydreamed about the many summers his family spent here. Tyler and Amy literally grew up here. They first visited Red River 10 months after Amy was born. Tyler was three and spent the better part of each day fishing in the trout pond right outside the very window that Alan was gazing out from. The peace and relaxation that Alan and Carol experienced was rivaled only by the adventures that the kids experienced every summer since.

While Alan felt a sense of sadness that neither of their children were with them this year, he still felt the profound sense of peace as he watched the young family of deer in the twilight of early morning.

Alan's thoughts quickly drifted back to the issue that ruined his sleep last night. For the first time in the 15 years he had served as the head of Lakeview Christian Academy, he was concerned about the school's future. And he was also concerned about his own future.

Just three days earlier, the Lakeview Christian Academy board was meeting for the final time before summer break. June is also the end of the school's fiscal year, so the June meeting was always longer, affording time to look back on the year completed as well as look forward to the year ahead.

The reality is Lakeview Christian was in financial trouble. The past two years started a trend that, if not reversed, would likely be the demise of the private school. There were so many moving parts, and at times, it seemed so complicated. But the bottom line was the school simply was not taking in enough money to operate and would soon run out of reserves to keep it afloat.

This was not what Alan had imagined when he became the founding headmaster of the school. Before accepting this role, both he and Carol had taught in numerous schools after graduating from Baylor University in the early 90s. Both had always been passionate about teaching, and when the opportunity to serve Lakeview Christian came along, they were all in.

Alan would never describe himself as a businessman, and he admittedly struggles with the business side of running the school. But he also knows that he is just like the vast majority of other heads of school. It is his passion for education and commitment to excellence that got him the job, not his business acumen. In retrospect, Alan sometimes wondered why teachers, and church pastors for that matter, aren't better educated about the business side of the institutions they end up running.

Fortunately, Lakeview Christian's board has plenty of business savvy. The board is small, seven members in total, with four members serving lifetime roles as founding board members. Alan could still hear Bill Irving's voice from the meeting the other night, booming over the board table stating in harsh terms that LCA was headed for bankruptcy.

It all came down to the finances and making the model work. Alan sat in silence and recounted the stress-filled meeting from just three days before...

June 29, 5:59 p.m., Lakeview Christian Academy Boardroom, McKinney, Texas

Bill Irving is the board chair and has been for all 15 years the school has existed. He is also one of the permanent founding members. He's been involved with LCA since the beginning because he had young grandchildren in McKinney and was adamant that they attend a private Christian school. Now, Bill is 68 years old and, although he is unaware of it, slightly hard of hearing. So, he speaks extra loud believing that everyone shares his struggle to hear discussion around the table.

"I'm officially calling this meeting to order. Can I get a second?" Bill shouted, drawing half smiles from the rest in the room not believing he was speaking so loudly. Mary Samson, another one of the four founding board members, quickly responded by asking, "Shouldn't we wait for Stan?" Bill bellowed back, "We all know what time these meetings start. Is Stan's time more important than the rest of ours?"

Bill is a retired Army general and, consequently, runs a tight ship when it comes to board meetings. Bill spent most of his military career on the finance side of the Army. He keeps his CPA status current and runs a small accounting business in McKinney providing services to local small businesses. Therefore, Bill tends to view everything through an accounting lens.

Mike Arnold chimed in, "I'll second the motion to call the meeting to order," just as Stan Grimes walked into the room, slightly miffed that the meeting was starting without him even though he arrived at 6:00 p.m. sharp.

"All in favor?" shouted Bill. "Aye," said all seven board members in unison.

Bill began with an overview of the meeting. "We have a lot to cover tonight, and I know we are all anxious to get started on the Fourth of July break. Let me just say right up front that our financial position has continued to decline, and the future looks dismal from that perspective. It all comes down to revenue and expenses, and our expenses continue to exceed our revenue. If we can't get this ship righted quickly, Lakeview Christian will sink."

After the weight of Bill's monologue soaked in over a moment of silence, Catherine Porter, the eternal optimist on the board, was the first to speak. "Now Bill, since I joined this board four years ago, we have been hearing about how the school's death is imminent. Yet, somehow, we pull it together and make ends meet. I trust that God will keep the mission alive for the sake of our kids and community."

"I appreciate your positive outlook and faithfulness, but neither your confidence nor prayer, Catherine, will pay the bills we have before us!" Bill shot back.

"Now, now. Let's keep this civil. We are all on the same team here and want the same outcome for Lakeview Christian," offered Mike Arnold in an attempt to bring down the level of tension in the room. Mike is the board's peacekeeper who hates conflict. "Bill, we hear you loud and clear," drawing half smiles again from the others, "that the current trend is unacceptable. We all know that something must change if LCA is to survive. Let's all be respectful of one another and the opinions we express."

Bill looked miffed, "There is a time for calm, and there is a time to act. We need action now."

Larry Dolan spoke next. "I am pleased to see some passion in the room tonight. We are all smart and successful people outside of this boardroom, and I have confidence that we can come up with a solution if we put our collective wisdom—and prayer," Larry looked over at Catherine and nodded, "to work."

Larry is also a founding board member and still an active parent of three kids at LCA. He is also the CEO of a large technology company in north Texas, and the Dolans are arguably one of the wealthiest families in the school. "Our circumstances simply will require us to consider doing things differently in the future. Let's throw out some ideas," Larry suggested as he stood and walked to the whiteboard in the conference room.

"Our options are pretty simple," Larry continued. "We can either increase revenue, or we can decrease expenses. It really boils down to some combination of these two actions." Larry is a charismatic and credible business leader who exudes confidence as he speaks. It is easy for people to understand why he is so successful.

Larry drew a simple grid on the whiteboard with two columns—one titled *expense* and the other titled *revenue*. "So, let's start brainstorming on both sides of the financial equation. Let's hear some ideas."

Mary spoke first. "We could raise tuition."

As Larry began to write her suggestion under the revenue column, Jane Littleton, the newest and youngest board member responded, "We raise tuition every year and never seem to get anywhere. The more we raise tuition, the more students leave us because we become unaffordable. We are just spinning our wheels."

Larry turned to Jane and politely chided her. "Jane, we are brainstorming ideas here, not making decisions. Let's all please add to the list for a while before we start crossing off ideas."

With that instruction, the group brainstormed several ideas on both the expense and revenue sides of the chart. On the expense side were ideas such as laying off some faculty, refinancing the school's current debt, slow paying some of the school's vendors, reducing the amount of tuition assistance given to lower-income families, and asking LCA administrators to take pay cuts.

On the revenue side were ideas that included raising tuition, adding extra fees to cover some items historically covered by tuition, growing enrollment, tapping into next year's tuition revenue by incentivizing some families to pay early, and raising additional money through fundraising activities.

Everyone participated in the discussion, including Alan, although he was beginning to feel sick to his stomach as the expense side of the chart was filled out. Alan dreaded the prospect of implementing all but one of the ideas on the expense side. He already knew of four faculty members and one administrator who were demanding pay increases. Laying off teachers would send the wrong message to the rest of the LCA faculty and staff, not to mention the community. And, although he was willing to lead by example, he also knew that he would likely lose some of his most trusted administrators if he asked them to take pay cuts.

The one area of expense reduction Alan supported was the possibility of restructuring the school's long-term debt. Six years ago, LCA borrowed $12 million to build a new gymnasium and high school classroom building. Servicing that debt was a significant factor contributing to LCA's financial challenges.

On the revenue side, Alan was open to all of the ideas. But he also knew that Bill had a strong opinion about fundraising that most on the board were unwilling to challenge. Bill believes that a private school should never rely on annual fundraising for operational needs. Rather, a school should be able to operate within its budget, solely determined by tuition. And, for the first 13 years while LCA was growing and adding grade levels, the books had balanced without the need for fundraising. The past two years, however, were a different story, resulting in cumulative deficits of over half a million dollars.

As the discussion of the ideas on both sides of the chart unfolded, Alan's stomach situation worsened. Bill pushed hard on the expense side and fought hard against the prospect of leaning on annual fundraising to balance the budget. In fact, at times it seemed as if

Bill would rather watch the school fail than to reverse his view on fundraising.

When the meeting adjourned at 8:30 p.m., no final decisions were made, but Alan was given his marching orders to put together an expense reduction and revenue growth plan that included all of the ideas the board had brainstormed earlier. In addition, the board agreed—Bill reluctantly—to consider the prospect of adding fundraising to the mix in the future as a means of growing operational revenue.

As the board slowly dissipated with well wishes for summer vacations that were about to begin, it seemed to Alan that no one wanted to engage with him in conversation about the tasks at hand. This added to Alan's already blue mood and rising anxiety.

What a way to start my vacation, he thought. *I wonder if I will even have a job when I get back.*

July 2, 6:14 a.m., Red River, New Mexico

As Alan came out of his deep thoughts of that board meeting, he realized it was much lighter outside. The family of deer had moved on, and now he could see fishermen staking out the most coveted spots around the pond. Alan wondered if any of them were experiencing a crisis or the overwhelming weight of responsibility that he was. *Probably not,* he concluded and then stood up to refill his coffee mug.

When Alan returned to his seat, he was feeling frustration for letting pressures from the school invade his retreat time. "That's enough!" he said out loud, "I'm going to put this out of my mind and have a nice time this week with Carol." As if on command, his mood started to lift. He decided that he would begin this morning with a vigorous hike up the face of the mountain. He knew if he left now, he could be back down by the time Carol awoke. Little did he know that work issues would become the primary focus of his vacation in the coming days.

Alan walked out the door at 6:30 a.m. and was off to the base of the mountain, just a short three-minute walk. It was a cool, crisp morning, and the skies looked clear blue. *This is why we love the mountains in summer,* he thought as he imagined the scorching, hot weather back home in Texas. There was no one else in sight as he began to trudge up the snowless ski slope ahead. About 100 yards later, Alan was reminded that he had not yet acclimated to the altitude. He rested his lungs for a minute and then continued the climb.

The beauty surrounding him, along with the cool, fresh air, helped to further clear his head. Soon he fell into a comfortable pace as his mind drifted to the memories of making this climb with Amy and Tyler so many times before.

About 45 minutes later and about two-thirds of the way up the mountain, Alan stepped on some loose rocks on a steep slope that slipped out from under his right foot. His ankle turned hard, and he fell to both knees, sliding down the slope about 10 feet. Alan winced from the pain and cursed out loud.

He rolled over to a sitting position to do an assessment of his condition. Both knees were scraped up and bleeding. Only superficial wounds though; nothing that bandages and antiseptic couldn't handle. His right ankle, however, was the problem. It was already rapidly swelling and extremely painful to the touch.

Alan scooted down the slope a little farther to a slightly less steep area in order to test the ankle. When he tried to stand, the pain was unbearable. Alan quickly sat back down to make a plan. His first realization was that he hadn't bothered telling Carol, or anyone for that matter, that he was going for a hike. "That was pretty dumb!" he said out loud.

He did, however, bring his cell phone, more out of habit than as a precaution. He pulled the phone from his backpack to check for a signal. Red River is not quite as modern as many of the other Colorado ski resorts. There were no cell towers on the mountain, but perhaps the base towers would at least provide a weak signal.

His phone showed the weakest of weak signals, fluctuating between one bar and the no signal icon. After trying three times unsuccessfully to place a call to Carol's cell phone, Alan decided to try sending her a text message. Three minutes after sending the message, his phone signaled that the message had been delivered. Great news! He sent 3 more short messages to her phone over the next 10 minutes providing instructions and his approximate location. Now it was just a matter of time before help arrived.

Alan sat back and relaxed. Looking down the mountain at this time of morning availed a beautiful view of the town of Red River. So many great memories. Alan retrieved his water bottle and rehydrated. As he was putting the bottle back in his backpack, he heard a man's voice just below him. "Hey, are you okay?" asked the stranger hiking the same path as Alan.

Rounding the bend about 100 feet below where Alan was seated was another hiker. Alan waved and answered quickly, "As a matter of fact, no! I twisted my ankle pretty badly and can't stand on it."

Alan gave a quick recount of his story to the man, including the texts he sent his wife that would likely not be read for another hour or so when she wakes up.

The man introduced himself. "I'm Gene Benson. I have a place in the upper valley. I am the only one in my family who enjoys these early morning hikes." Alan smiled at him and in turn introduced himself with a similar story.

"There is no chance I am going to leave you here in the middle of this slope. Maybe I can help you get to a more comfortable spot and then go for help?" offered Gene.

"Thank you! You are a Godsend happening on to me here," replied Alan. "Do you think you could help me get down to that plateau in the shade of those trees?" pointing downslope 50 feet or so. Gene helped Alan to stand on his good leg, and the two of them hobbled to the spot Alan had indicated.

Gene rolled a couple of logs over from the woods, one for Alan to lean against and the other to elevate his injured ankle. Once Alan was looking comfortable, Gene sat down next to him to chat. "I have been bringing my family here for years. We love Red River," offered Gene.

Alan reciprocated with his story and affection for the mountain town, and then asked, "Where is home when you're not in Red River?"

Gene replied, "We live in McKinney, Texas. How about you?"

Alan couldn't believe his ears. "We live in McKinney too! We moved there from Amarillo about 15 years ago. What do you do in McKinney, Gene?"

"I work in the nonprofit world. I am the executive director of Collin County Family Services, a human services organization serving McKinney and surrounding towns. How about you?" Gene asked.

"I, too, am in the nonprofit world. I am the headmaster at Lakeview Christian Academy."

Alan and Gene proceeded to make some common connections and discovered that they live just a few miles apart in McKinney. Gene then stood up and looked up the mountain. "I see you have plenty of water, Alan. If you are okay here for a while, I'll go on to the top and call the ranger's office for help. I can probably make it in about 15 minutes or so. Once I make the call, I will hike back down and wait with you."

Alan now felt embarrassed for all the kindness and help from Gene, "You are kind, Gene. Thank you. But you don't need to hike back down here. I will be fine until the ranger arrives."

"Don't be ridiculous!" Gene replied with a warm smile. "What could possibly be more important than helping out my new friend and neighbor in McKinney?"

With that, Gene set off up the mountain with the promise to return.

Alan laid back and relaxed as well as he could sitting on rocks leaning against a log with a throbbing ankle. In spite of the pain and frustration, Alan was in pretty good spirits given his good fortune being discovered by his new friend and rescuer, Gene. *What an amazing coincidence that we live so near one another in McKinney and should end up meeting in the middle of the New Mexico Rocky Mountains!* he thought.

Alan's worries from earlier this morning suddenly seemed less important. He now wondered how he could ever thank Gene enough for his help.

Alan glanced at his phone again and saw the time was 7:51 a.m.—still at least 40 minutes before Carol would likely see his texts. Alan then sent one more text explaining his encounter with Gene.

The next half hour was uneventful and passed slowly. No other human hikers passed by, but another family of deer did emerge from the forest. The large doe eyed Alan cautiously and eventually determined he was no threat to her family, and they proceeded to cross the rocky slope in front of him. Just as they were near the forest on the other side of the slope, the doe became spooked by a strange noise and darted into the woods with her family right behind her.

Seconds later, Alan heard the noise that spooked the deer. It was an all-terrain vehicle coming down the mountain. The engine noise grew louder and eventually Alan could see the red vehicle with rangers' markings making the turn and heading directly toward him. As it approached, Alan could see Gene sitting beside the ranger who was driving the ATV.

The ride down the mountain took only about 20 minutes. Near the base, Alan's cell signal was strong enough to place a call to Carol. The phone rang four times before a sleepy Carol answered. "Hello, Alan? Why are you calling me?" It was obvious that Carol had slept in a bit later than normal. Alan was envious of Carol's ability to sleep.

Alan explained to Carol what had happened and asked her to drive over to meet him at the mountain medical clinic. When Carol arrived, she was greeted by Gene. "Mrs. Morgan? Hi. I'm Gene Benson. I met your husband this morning on my hike. Unfortunately, his hike was already over when we met."

An hour and a half later, Alan was discharged from the clinic with a pair of crutches and a boot to protect his severely sprained right ankle. "We just can't thank you enough, Gene," said Carol. "If you hadn't found Alan, I'd hate to think what could have happened to him before I could have gotten help. You must let us repay you by having you to dinner." With Carol at the wheel of their Chevy Tahoe, they drove Gene back to his car. Before parting they exchanged contact information and agreed to get together the following evening for dinner.

The rest of the day for Alan was less active. Doctor's orders were to remain horizontal and keep his ankle elevated and iced. With a healthy dose of pain medication working its way into his bloodstream, Alan laid back on the couch and watched the ceiling fan spin. He recounted his morning and meeting Gene. Aside from being eternally grateful for their chance meeting, he liked Gene. As best he could guess, Gene was a few years older than him, maybe mid 50s. But Alan suddenly realized he hadn't learned much of anything about Gene. In fact, Alan had been so consumed with his own situation that he simply neglected to ask Gene anything about his personal life.

Alan could remember a few things that Gene had offered when they first met. Gene lives in McKinney and runs a social service nonprofit—Collin County Family Services, he recalled. With that, Alan grabbed his iPad from the nearby coffee table and Googled *Collin County Family Services*.

The website for CCFS was impressive. Alan quickly reviewed the mission and services. CCFS had been around for 16 years, roughly the same age as Lakeview Christian. Yet Alan was not familiar with the organization. It provides relief and support to low-income families in Collin County, helping some to break out of poverty and others through transitional times of unemployment. They provide direct financial assistance to help pay for utilities, food from a food pantry, temporary housing, job skills training, and a myriad of other support services.

Alan next clicked on the Collin County Family Services Leadership button. At the top was a picture of Gene. Alan read through his vitae. Gene came to CCFS seven years ago after serving as a fundraising consultant for 25 years. Gene and his wife, Karen, relocated to McKinney from St. Louis to take this position.

Putting the iPad on his lap, Alan gazed back up at the ceiling fan and thought about Gene's background. *A fundraising consultant for most of his career.* He wondered how that role could possibly have prepared Gene to lead a social service agency like CCFS.

Now more curious than ever, Alan looked up the annual report for CCFS. After reading through the agency's accomplishments for the previous fiscal year, he scrolled to the financials section. CCFS had an annual budget of $12.5 million: *CCFS is a significant mission,* Alan thought. He then reviewed the sources of revenue. About a fourth, a little over $3 million, came from government sources. Alan paused a moment to consider this finding. He was surprised so little came from government sources. He would have expected that number to account for nearly all of the budget for a social service organization.

Alan read on. The rest of CCFS's revenue came from local fundraising. Almost $9 million in annual fundraising from sources such as grants and events, but the kicker was that the largest source of fundraising revenue came from "Individuals." Just over $6 million of the $9 million raised last year came from individual donors! In disbelief, Alan half wondered if this might be a typo.

Scrolling to the next page, Alan next reviewed the growth path of CCFS for the past five years. He quickly learned that CCFS had more than doubled its annual revenue in the last five years. His eyes went right to the revenue chart showing the growth of each revenue source. Most revenue sources were fairly static, showing modest growth year over year. Interestingly, government funding had actually gone down over the past five years. But the one source that screamed to be noticed was the "Individuals" category.

Five years ago, CCFS raised about $975,000 from Individuals. Each year since, that specific category had grown by more than $1 million. Amazing! Alan once again laid down the iPad and watched the fan above his head, trying to imagine what Gene was doing in the "Individuals" category of fundraising. After a few minutes, Alan thought he had it figured out. Gene must have a couple of "sugar-daddy" donors who have been funding his agency.

Alan decided to make some notes to discuss with Gene, should the opportunity avail itself in conversation over dinner the next evening. But as he began to write, the side effects of the pain medication were kicking in, causing Alan to drift off to sleep.

Carol checked on Alan throughout the afternoon and kept ice on the ankle without disturbing his slumber. At one point, Carol noticed a note pad on Alan's chest sticking out from the blanket that was covering him. She gently slid the pad out from under the blanket to make him more comfortable, and then glanced at his notes before she put it down on the table.

Gene Benson—former fundraising consultant

7 years; 2x budget

Gov't funding down

Individuals? 6M+—How?

Ethics of fundraising? School?

Carol woke Alan in the early evening to give him more medication and some nourishment. Alan was groggy from deep sleep but felt better rested. As his head began to clear, the events from earlier in the day seemed like a dream. He was quickly reminded of reality when he pulled back the blanket to see his bruised, bandaged knees and swollen ankle.

Carol fixed Alan some soup and sat down next him to help him eat given his angle of incline on the couch. As she fed him, she asked about his notes on the pad she had found on his chest. Alan looked confused for a moment and then recalled he had started making notes before falling asleep. "Oh yeah. I decided to look up Gene and learn more about him, since I was so self-centered this morning on the mountain. What an impression I must have given him."

Carol offered, "I think, under the circumstances, Gene understood your 'it's all about me' attitude this morning. Besides, you will have the opportunity to show him otherwise tomorrow evening. By the way, I invited the Bensons to come here for dinner since you will still likely be somewhat physically challenged. So, what did you learn about Gene this morning?"

"He is a fundraiser! So, we should guard our wallets tomorrow night," joked Alan. "Most of his career he consulted with nonprofits to help them raise money. And, based on his track record as executive director of Collin County Family Services, his fundraising skills have served him and their mission well."

Raising to the Challenge

PART II

It is paradoxical, yet true, to say, that the more we know, the more ignorant we become in the absolute sense, for it is only through enlightenment that we become conscious of our limitations. Precisely one of the most gratifying results of intellectual evolution is the continuous opening up of new and greater prospects.
– Nikola Tesla

July 3, 5:30 p.m., Red River, New Mexico

Carol was lighting a couple of candles when they heard knocking at the door. Alan was already on his crutches and near the door, wanting to be the one who greeted the Bensons. As Alan was opening the door, his left crutch slid out from under his arm. Gene saw Alan falling and quickly caught him. "We have to quit meeting like this," shot Gene, after which they all shared a hearty belly laugh.

Once inside and recomposed, Alan extended his right hand to Karen. "It is so nice to meet you." As Karen gripped Alan's right hand, his right crutch slipped a little on the entryway carpet. Karen quickly grabbed Alan's arm to prevent him from falling. The belly laughing recommenced while Gene, Karen, and Carol all helped Alan to the couch. "I think I now fully understand how you came to injure yourself yesterday. You had better stay here the rest of the evening," joked Gene.

The four sat down together for drinks and appetizers, then spent the next hour getting to know each other. In spite of Alan's determination to ask more questions of Gene and Karen, he caught himself speaking more than listening. Gene had a way about him that was easy to be around. He was disarming. Gene seemed genuinely interested in everything Alan and Carol had to say.

"Alright. You have heard entirely too much about our lives. Tell us your story," Alan finally said. Gene deferred to Karen to speak. "Well, for the first 25 years of our marriage and most of our children's lives at home, Gene was a road warrior. He worked for a consulting firm that helped nonprofits conduct capital campaigns and, as such, lived on the road 80 percent of the time. While it was hard not having him around," Karen said as she patted Gene's knee and looked over at him affectionately, "we all knew his work was important. Gene has helped change so many lives for good through his work. So, I stayed home during those years and tended to our children and home."

It was Gene's turn to talk. "I worked very hard as a consultant and had the privilege of working with many great nonprofit missions. And while we reaped the benefits of millions of frequent flyer miles, I do regret missing so much of our kids' lives growing up," Gene said as he returned the glance to Karen.

"In the end," Gene continued, "I burned out. I knew I had to come off the road and plug back into my family. And that's when the opportunity at Collin County Family Services came along. I have always had a heart for the needs of low-income families and the homeless. In addition to countless private schools and arts and cultural organizations, I had worked with dozens of similar social service agencies training boards and raising money. I just fell in love with the mission at CCFS."

Gene's mention of private schools did not slip by Alan. In fact, sirens went off in Alan's head. But Alan didn't want to be disrespectful by bringing the conversation so quickly back to himself just yet.

Gene and Karen told the Morgans all about their grown children's lives—and their hope for a grandchild in the not-too-distant future. Just as the conversation was reaching a lull, Carol announced that dinner was ready.

Gene immediately acted to help Alan get to his one good foot and over to the chair at the end of the table. Carol had already set up a stool with a pillow on it to keep Alan's leg elevated. All seated around the table, Alan asked if he could say a blessing before dinner. Not knowing the faith background of the Bensons, Alan glanced to see their reaction. Both nodded and bowed their heads naturally.

Alan offered a short blessing and gave special thanks for Gene's help and unexpected kindness. When he said "Amen," he noticed the Bensons kept their heads bowed for a moment longer and then made the sign of the cross. "Are you part of a parish in McKinney?" asked Alan. Gene chuckled and said, "I guess that our Catholic upbringing is obvious. Yes, we have been part of St. Gabriel's since moving to McKinney." Alan, also chuckling, offered, "That's great. We have been a part of several churches over the years. We consider ourselves Christian mutts and friends of all Christian faiths."

Over dinner, the conversation remained light. The two couples discussed their mutual fondness for Red River and the fun things they had done over the years.

After dinner, Gene helped Alan back to the couch and just the two of them sat over cups of coffee while Karen helped Carol clear the dishes.

Alan started the conversation. "Gene, I am intrigued about your fundraising background and your work with schools. To say that I am fundraising challenged would be a gross understatement. In fact, at Lakeview Christian, we do very little fundraising."

Gene listened and nodded while Alan spoke and then responded only when he believed Alan was through. "Well, Alan, that story sounds familiar. Most schools tend to rely on tuition alone in the early years of existence. But, given that LCA is 15 years old, I would have guessed you needed to raise some money to supplement tuition revenue in order to operate the school. How have you managed?" Gene asked.

"Well," Alan responded while smiling with a little embarrassment, "to be honest, we really haven't managed lately. For the past two fiscal years, our expenses have exceeded our revenue, and our reserves are quickly vanishing. And I get it, That's no way to run a railroad."

Gene returned the smile in a way that let Alan know that he was not judging and then said, "May I ask why LCA doesn't do more fundraising?"

"A few reasons," Alan began. "Probably the biggest reason is that my board chair is adamantly opposed to fundraising for operational needs and believes that tuition should always be set at a level that matches our annual expenses. He questions whether fundraising is even ethical for a private school. He is also somewhat of a bully, so he is rarely challenged on anything by other board members."

Gene nodded and smiled even bigger as Alan filled him in on Bill, his hard-of-hearing board chair.

Alan continued, "Beyond the board's lack of appetite for fundraising, we simply don't know how to fundraise. Can I ask how you have seen it work in other private schools?"

Again, Gene paused and looked down at his lap for a moment. To Alan, it appeared he was gathering his thoughts and thinking carefully about his choice of words. Finally, in an even-toned voice, Gene said, "I want to be very cautious here, Alan. I don't know all of the circumstances surrounding your challenges at LCA. Therefore, it would be irresponsible of me to take up a position and counsel you in a direction that might be contradictory to your board's position. It would be like the medical clinic physician yesterday prescribing treatment without even looking at your ankle."

Alan nodded, showing he understood the analogy perfectly.

"With that on the table, let me offer you some facts about the broader private school world," Gene paused again to make sure Alan was still tracking. "With few exceptions, all private schools in America require some supplementary funding in order to pay for annual operating costs. The truth is, the actual cost of educating students most often is higher than many parents are willing to pay. Also, all private schools must raise capital from time to time in order to keep pace with growth and demand for quality facilities."

Alan could not conceal his shock. His eyes opened wider, and his jaw dropped open a bit. Gene noticed Alan's reaction and reached over to put his right hand on Alan's shoulder. "Why do I feel like I just ruined Christmas for you by telling you there is no Santa?" Gene asked with a smile.

Alan caught himself and shook his head as if to throw off a spell. "Are you sure about that? I mean, for the first 13 years, LCA operated within our tuition-revenue-sized budget. And we have never had a capital campaign. Are we just better at this than most schools?" asked Alan in a somewhat skeptical tone.

"Well, maybe," replied Gene in an equally skeptical but playful tone, "but I bet during those 13 years you were managing into growth in enrollment, right?" Alan nodded as the gears in his brain were turning to follow. Gene continued, "Once enrollment begins to plateau, the reality of rising costs and tuition thresholds begin to set in."

"So, what you are saying is that the deficits we have experienced recently are normal from your perspective, given we are not raising funds to help. But why haven't we needed to raise capital?"

"Well, I'm not sure. Let me ask you a few more questions. Where did the land and buildings come from to start LCA?"

Alan answered quickly, "They were donated to us by one of our founding board members. He purchased the land that already had some usable buildings on it from a local church."

"Aha! So, you have done capital fundraising!" shot Gene. "Where did the other buildings come from?"

"Eight years after LCA opened, we borrowed $12.5 million to pay for the construction of a gym and upper-school building. This was completed just in time for the eighth-grade class to move in the following year," answered Alan.

"Did anyone donate any money for the buildings?" asked Gene.

"No. But a few board members did help guarantee the loan. LCA was still relatively new and did not have collateral to secure that size of a loan."

"Okay. Yet more evidence of fundraising!" added Gene.

Alan looked confused, "I have never thought of either of those things as fundraising. How do you figure?" Alan asked this question with complete sincerity.

Gene began, "I'm certain that the board member who donated the land did so to help launch a great new private Christian school mission. He probably also took the tax deduction for the charitable gift he made to LCA. And, even though there weren't official donations to pay for the new buildings eight years later, board members took on the risk that the school was unable to take on. Without that act of support, LCA could not have borrowed the money, right?"

"Alright, I'm beginning to track with you now," Alan shared while nodding. "What you're saying is that we have received supplementary support. We just didn't think of it that way."

"Yes, to some degree. Without that support, you may have had to lease space initially, which, in turn, would have driven your operating costs higher. If you could not have borrowed the money to build eight years ago, you either would have had to raise it some other way or else not build. And if you did not build, you would not have had space to accommodate the graduating eighth graders and, consequently, lost significant tuition revenue." Gene walked through this sequence deliberately, but in no way did he seem to speak down to Alan.

Gene finished with this, "My point is that private schools almost always require supplemental support beyond tuition revenue. Even though LCA has not deliberately sought charitable giving as a necessary element of its financial model, the unsolicited gifts are what allowed the school's financial model to work. Accepting this basic concept may help you and your board come to terms with fundraising in the future."

As Gene spoke those final words, Carol and Karen were sitting down to join them. Alan's mind was working hard to take in all that Gene had shared. Carol looked at him and said, "Are you okay, honey? You look a bit confused."

Alan again shook his head and smiled. "In a last few minutes, Gene just blew up everything that I thought I knew about the money side of Lakeview Christian."

Karen cut in, "Well, I'm glad you two have so much to talk about. Carol and I have planned a shopping excursion to Taos the day after tomorrow. Maybe you two can get together and talk more?"

Alan graciously replied, "I'm sure Gene has seen too much of me already and has far more interesting things to do than to teach a crippled head of school the ropes of fundraising."

Before Gene could answer for himself, Karen quickly added, "No, he doesn't! And besides, the only way Carol will go shopping with me is if there is someone here to keep an eye on Alan."

They all chuckled, and then Gene readily agreed. "If you would like, I will bring over lunch Wednesday, and we can spend the afternoon together."

After some final small talk between the two couples about the Fourth of July parade scheduled for the next day and festivities in the town the next 24 hours, the new friends said goodnight.

Once Gene and Karen were in their car, Karen quickly asked Gene, "So, what do you think?" Gene offered without hesitation, "I like them both. It's amazing we live so near one another in McKinney and have been vacationing for years so near one another in Red River, yet never met."

"I sure like Carol. She and I have so much in common. There is a straightforwardness about her that I like very much. I am looking forward to spending the day with her on Wednesday. I hope you don't mind that I committed you to take care of Alan," Karen offered a bit sheepishly.

Gene laughed. "Not at all. I like Alan as well. He has been through a lot in the last two days with his ankle. Alan also has a delicate situation to deal with at his school. But he is sincere and seems truly interested in figuring out how to solve his problems, unlike some of my clients back in the consulting days. I think I can help him."

Inside the Morgans' home, Alan and Carol were having a similar discussion, although it was Alan who spoke first. "What a Godsend to meet Gene like I did. I really like him. And, even though we are relatively close in age, he seems so much wiser."

Carol quickly responded, "You are pretty wise yourself, Dr. Morgan, but I know what you mean. He just has a way about him. He is not a know-it-all or arrogant in any way, yet he seems to know so much. I'm glad you two are hitting it off. I like Karen, too."

Fourth of July, Red River, New Mexico

Alan woke up early again, but not from the stress of work. Rather, the pain medication he had been on put him out early the night before, just after the Bensons left. Alan hobbled to his normal seat in the family room with one crutch and a mug of coffee in the other hand. *I think I'm finally getting the hang of getting around*, he thought proudly. Now comfortable and with his right ankle resting on a pillow, he gazed out the front window at the familiar scene. There was that family of deer again, peacefully roaming behind the pond. What a way to start the day.

Throughout the morning, Alan's mind was retracing the years at LCA, and he thought of several other situations where external support was provided to help the school. *We have actually been doing some serious fundraising for years and never realized it*, thought Alan in bewilderment.

Alan was beginning to understand that the only truly viable solution in the future was to increase fundraising revenue and take some strain off of tuition revenue. He decided to grab a pad of paper and pen and begin to make a list of the external fundraising support LCA had received in the past, already anticipating a showdown with his board chair in the weeks ahead.

The rest of the morning was peaceful and relaxing. At noon, Alan and Carol walked a block and a half to Main Street to watch the Fourth of July parade. It felt good to get out of the house and move a little, albeit on crutches. Red River still maintained the tradition of celebrating the Fourth in the same way it had been done for decades. Classic cars, fire trucks, high school bands, drill teams, and the likes all paraded down the main drag throwing candy to the kids and waving to the spectators lining both sides of the street.

As a large group of military veterans were marching behind a drum and fife team, Alan suddenly caught sight of Gene. He wore a veteran's cap and proudly walked beside his fellow veterans. "Man," whispered Alan in Carol's ear, "is there anything Gene hasn't done?" They both chuckled and then waved to get Gene's attention. When Gene saw them, he shouted, "Great to see you in a vertical position," and then smiled warmly.

That evening Alan and Carol relaxed on their deck and had their own Fourth of July backyard cookout. Carol assumed Alan's usual duties at the grill since he still had the burden of a boot and crutches. Over dinner Carol asked Alan how he was feeling. Alan replied without even thinking, "The pain isn't too bad anymore, and now that I am getting the hang of these crutches, I feel a little less helpless."

Carol smiled at Alan and said, "I didn't really mean how are you *feeling*, although I am happy to hear the pain is improving. I meant, how is your state of mind around the school's financial challenges?"

"Oh, sorry," replied Alan a bit embarrassed. "Well, I've slept much better the last two nights. But that might be the result of the drugs you have been making me take," he said grinning. "Seriously, I do think that getting some distance between us and LCA has helped me regain some perspective."

"How do you mean?" urged Carol.

"Well, for one, I think the school's financial solution is complex and will require change on several fronts. But I am becoming convinced that we have been mistaken in our position on annual fundraising," said Alan as he sat back and sipped on his cold drink.

"Okay. Where did that come from?"

As Alan began to form the first word of his answer, Carol knew exactly what he was about to say and said it out loud with him, "Gene Benson!" They chuckled together, and then Alan shot back, "Jinx!" They laughed some more as they suddenly both missed Amy and Tyler. How many hundreds of times had one of the kids said that when any two of them accidentally spoke in unison.

"I am happy that you met Gene, despite the less-than-ideal circumstances. You know, neither of us have made a new friend in years. I must admit, it's kind of fun to get to know someone new. Maybe the four of us can keep this going when we get back home."

Alan had already been thinking along the same lines.

July 5, Red River, New Mexico

Alan awoke early again and repeated his morning routine. Coffee, couch, window, deer, and so on. This morning, however, he felt energized. He slept well and without the aid of painkillers. But the real reason for Alan's mood was that Gene was bringing lunch and planning to spend the afternoon with him.

Not wanting to seem unprepared nor completely ignorant about fundraising when Gene arrived, Alan decided to take the morning to prepare. He had his iPad handy along with note paper and pen. He wrote at the top of the first page, FUNDRAISING IDEAS.

Alan had some familiarity with fundraising. He and Carol give to several fundraisers every year and even attend a few events. He started making a list of possible fundraising activities under the heading he had written.

- Christmas wrap sales
- Car wash
- Magazine subscriptions

He recalled students from other schools in the area knocking on their door and pedaling these kinds of things. But, thinking through these activities, he concluded that something on a larger scale would be required. So, he added a few more ideas.

- Golf outing

- Gala
- Auction
- 10K race

Now, these activities had potential. While Alan did not really know how to execute these kinds of events, he thought Gene would be impressed with his head start on the brainstorming process.

Next, Alan headed a separate note page with each activity, starting with GOLF OUTING.

Under the heading he added the subheadings REVENUE and EXPENSES and proceeded to list possible items under each. "Maybe I know more about fundraising than I thought," Alan said out loud. He listed under the revenue heading entry fees, hole sponsors, and contest add-ons. Under the expense side he listed golf course rental, gift bags and contents, and catering.

Alan's confidence was growing with every item he added to the list. He didn't really know what dollar figures to write down for either revenue or expenses. Gene could help him with that. After all, that is probably part of the value a consultant brings to a school like Lakeview Christian.

Alan completed this process for the other events he had listed and then sat back proud of his work this morning. Gene will be pleased with my initiative here, he thought. Just then Carol emerged from the bedroom prepared for a day of shopping with Karen in Taos.

"Good morning, sweetheart!" exclaimed Alan.

Carol immediately noticed a much more enthusiastic tone in Alan's voice. "Well, good morning back to you, Mr. Cheerful. I guess someone is feeling better today," said Carol.

"As a matter of fact, I am. I feel like I am getting on top of our financial problems at LCA. My limited conversations with Gene have stimulated my thinking about fundraising. I even have a rough draft of a plan to show him today," said Alan proudly.

"Good for you. But remember, Gene is here on vacation, too. His idea of spending the afternoon may not be solving all of your financial problems," warned Carol. Carol always had better insight into these things than Alan.

Carol left a few minutes later to go pick up Karen. As Alan continued to sit and think, he realized Carol was right. Maybe he should focus on just being Gene's friend right now. *Why in the world would Gene want to take a day out of his vacation to take care of me and focus on my school problems?* he thought.

Alan rethought the day and decided he would not hit Gene with his fundraising plan. Instead, he would explore more things they have in common and work on building their friendship.

At 11:30 a.m. sharp, Gene knocked on the door. Immediately after knocking he turned the handle and opened the door to prevent Alan from having to get up and risk falling. "Hello, in there. I come bearing gifts of pizza, wings, and Dr. Pepper," announced Gene.

"Come in, come in. Hi, Gene! How are you?"

"Still more mobile than you I see," joked Gene. "Stay where you are. I've got this."

Gene unpacked the sacks containing their lunch on the coffee table and sat down facing Alan. "Good to see you looking stronger today. Soon you will be back on the mountain."

"I don't know about that, but I am doing much better. The swelling is down and the pain is almost gone. No more pain meds, so I have my mind back," Alan said while tapping his temple with his index finger.

Alan had the television on and tuned to World Cup Soccer. Brazil was playing Croatia and it was shaping up to be quite a match. Gene immediately took note and said, "I was hoping you were a sports fan. I wanted to see this matchup today. I love World Cup Soccer."

Alan and Gene sat together as two male friends eating pizza and chicken wings while watching the soccer match. They were both rapt, and aside from a comment about a player, team, or a great play, didn't say much for a while.

When the first half of the soccer match was complete, the score was tied at one. Both men agreed that this was a great matchup. Alan muted the commercials playing during the intermission and turned to Gene. "Carol and I continue to be surprised at all that you have done in your life. When did you serve in the military?"

Gene replied, "I enlisted in the Army right out of high school because I wanted to serve, but also to earn some college money. I never really saw any action during my tour, but I was honored to serve my country. We are here in Red River every year for the Fourth, so I get invited to walk with the other veterans in the parade. There are some real heroes in that group, and I am honored to walk beside them."

Alan listened intently as Gene spoke so sincerely about that chapter in his life. He could detect some emotion in his voice as he described his fellow veterans. Alan nodded and smiled warmly and said, "Whether you saw action or not is far less important than your decision to serve. While I never felt called to serve in the military, I have great admiration and respect for those who do. Thank you for your service." And, although that is often a sentiment expressed by complete strangers, Alan said it in an authentic way, and Gene's reaction registered Alan's message.

In an effort to lighten up the air, Alan then asked, "So, the next thing you will tell me is that you were a fundraiser in the Army."

Gene smiled and chuckled. "No, no. That came much later."

Gene and Alan hung out together all afternoon and talked about everything that came to mind—except for fundraising. They were fast becoming good friends with much in common. And, although Croatia ended up winning the soccer match in double overtime, they nearly forgot the match was on.

At 5:15 p.m., Karen and Carol walked in the front door with lots of shopping bags, immediately producing concerned looks on Gene's and Alan's faces. One bag, however, was filled with burgers, fries, and milkshakes for the guys—a smart and strategic move on the women's part. Their day of shopping was a similar kind of bonding experience. The four friends ate together, recounted their days, and then decided to play cards.

They were so busy laughing and playing cards that hours had flown by before anyone realized it. Finally, Carol glanced at the clock and said with some shock, "Oh my, do you all realize it is after eleven?"

As the Bensons and Morgans were hugging goodbyes at the front door, Alan handed Gene his fundraising work from early this morning and said, "Gene, if you have a few minutes tomorrow, would you mind looking over my plan? I hope I am thinking along the right track. I just thought you could help me file off the rough edges."

Gene agreed readily and took Alan's plan with him to review the next morning, indicating he would return the plans the next afternoon. Thirty minutes later, Alan was deep into a good night's sleep. His last thought before drifting off was the image of Gene reviewing the plan over coffee in the morning. He couldn't wait to get Gene's feedback.

But Alan couldn't be more wrong about the reaction Gene would give him, nor did he have any idea of the journey he had just embarked upon with Gene.

July 6, Red River, New Mexico

Alan slept in the next morning. In fact, when he did awaken, he thought that a power outage occurred during the night before that must have reset the clocks. The familiar red digital display read 8:47 a.m. Even more strange, Carol was already up and having her coffee. "Well, good morning, sleepyhead," she said. "I actually considered checking your pulse to make sure you were still with us."

Alan yawned and stretched, still a bit disoriented. "I haven't slept like that in years! I guess I am finally relaxing."

After two cups of coffee, his grogginess began to fade. Alan remembered that Gene was planning to review his fundraising plan this morning. He smiled while he sipped his third cup of coffee and wondered what Gene was thinking.

It wasn't until late afternoon that the phone rang. Alan picked it up before it could ring a second time and said hello before the handset was close to his mouth. It was Gene. "Hi, Alan! How's the ankle today?"

"Hi, Gene. Much better and feeling the need to get out of the house today—definitely have some cabin fever," replied Alan.

"Just what I was hoping to hear. You up for a crutch walk around the trout pond?"

"Absolutely!" said Alan with the excitement of a schoolboy.

Gene pulled in 10 minutes later, and Alan met him on the porch. Alan immediately noticed and was somewhat disappointed that Gene had nothing in his hands. Oh well, he thought—maybe his notes are in the car and he will grab them after our walk. The two men shook hands warmly and greeted each other.

Gene said, "Looks like another perfect afternoon in Red River. It would be a shame to waste it inside. Let's take a walk."

Alan shot back with "Hear, hear!"

As they started to make their way around the pond, Alan couldn't wait to open their discussion. "Gene, I'm dying to know what you thought of my ideas. Am I on the right track?"

Gene left a long pause before starting in. "Alan, I have been thinking all morning about how to have this conversation." Suddenly Alan was concerned. Gene continued, "You and I have become fast new friends these past few days but are still getting to know one another. I don't want to hurt your feelings or seem disrespectful."

Alan stopped walking and looked at Gene in the eyes. "Are you breaking up with me?" They both laughed, and it lightened the moment in such a way that the rest of the conversation would be easier.

After the laughter subsided, Gene went on, "As you know, I was a fundraising consultant most of my career. A critical element of doing my job well was establishing a healthy working relationship based on trust and speaking the truth, no matter how hard it is to say and hear. Right now, I am your friend first, not your consultant. But I can help you if you will permit me to step into the role of your consultant. I just want to be sure you want to hear what I have to say." Gene finished his speech and looked at Alan for his reaction.

Now it was Alan's turn. "Gene, I know we are new friends, but in a short time I have come to respect you and your knowledge of many things. I am one who believes that our meeting the other day on the mountain was providential. I believe God brought you into my life for a specific reason, and that reason, besides being my friend, may just be to educate my thick skull on fundraising. So, let me have it! Say it like it is! I might push back a bit if something sounds off, but I trust that you are only trying to help."

The two men shook hands spontaneously, as if to officially launch a new chapter in their relationship, and continued their journey around the trout pond.

Gene began with a request. "Alan, I only have a rudimentary understanding of your challenges so far. Give me a thumbnail of your circumstances."

Alan laid it out for Gene, "Well, I am projecting a $300,000 loss this year if nothing changes. We are down 18 students from last year, so tuition revenue will be down $180,000. In addition, my fixed costs will rise about $125,000. I know it sounds crazy that fixed costs can rise, but I have faculty and staff who expect and deserve modest increases in their compensation in addition to other cost increases tied to the rising cost of living. If we take that big of a loss this year, we will deplete our reserve fund, leaving nothing to address unplanned expenses." Alan looked at Gene indicating he was finished.

"Okay," Gene began, "that tells me what I need to know. The way I see it, Alan, is that you have both short-term and long-term challenges. And each challenge will require its own solution. Let's get busy."

After a brief period of silence, Alan asked with a half-smile, "Was I that far off the mark with the plans I sent home with you yesterday?"

Gene responded grinning back, "Your ideas for fundraising events are fine. Events are intuitive and the way almost every nonprofit gets started in fundraising. And doing events like you have outlined are fine in moderation, so long as you have reasonable expectations of what they can achieve and what problems they create."

Alan was confused. "I'm not sure I'm tracking with you Gene. What do you mean by 'problems events can create'?"

"Here comes some of the harsh stuff," warned Gene. "Most events are gimmicks designed to separate people from their money while masking the real cause to which the money will go. They are expensive to conduct and don't really yield a great return on the investment. Finally, events are absolutely not the right answer to your short-term challenge."

"Wow! That does sound a bit harsh, Gene," chided Alan. "Please say more."

They both chuckled before Gene continued. "You're right; that was intentionally harsh and cynical. Now that I have your attention, let's back up a few steps and start with the basic premise of fundraising. Alan, why do you think most nonprofit organizations raise funds?"

"Is this a trick question?" asked Alan rhetorically. "To fund all or part of their missions."

"Pretty simple, right? It's pretty easy to conclude that, if there is no fundraising, all or a part of the mission can't happen. There is a direct correlation between fundraising and mission outcomes. And every nonprofit organization wants to grow its mission. Therefore, every nonprofit organization needs to grow its funding. You tracking?" Alan nodded.

Gene continued, "So think for a moment about how a new nonprofit mission begins. Let's use a homeless shelter as an example. Someone is driven by a passion for the unmet need of caring for the homeless, and they launch a new nonprofit mission to address that unmet need. Where do you think the funding comes from to launch the new nonprofit?"

Alan thought a moment before responding, "Maybe the founder invests personally, or perhaps some seed money investors are lined up who also have passion for serving the homeless."

"Exactly right!" Gene took note that Alan looked pleased by his affirmation.

"And where will the ongoing funding come from to operate the homeless shelter?" asked Gene.

"From fundraising?"

"Right again! Every founder of a nonprofit mission quickly realizes that he or she must now become a fundraiser in order for the mission to survive and grow. Because, without fundraising, there is no mission. Do you think that anyone ever started a nonprofit organization because they have a passion for fundraising? Probably not!" added Gene before Alan tried to answer the rhetorical question. "The realization that the executive director must be a fundraiser always comes later and usually with some level of pain."

"I'm following you. In fact, I am probably going through that same realization right now."

Gene smiled at Alan and nodded. "You are the CEO of your business. Even though Lakeview Christian is a nonprofit school and ministry, it is still a business because it requires sustainable revenue to cover expenses in order to exist. Now, here's the kicker: the odd thing about the nonprofit sector is that its revenue sources are always different than the targets of the missions."

Gene let that last statement set in for a moment, and he could see Alan staring off into the distance thinking it through. Finally, Alan asked, "Can you say that one more time?"

Gene nodded patiently and began again, "In the for-profit world, the consumer of the service or product being sold is also almost always the source of revenue. Think of a product or service you regularly buy."

Alan offered, "How about Christina's Tex-Mex Restaurant?"

"Perfect! By the way, Karen and I love Christina's," replied Gene. "So, you probably visit Christina's because the food, service, and atmosphere are great. That is what Christina's strives to do: serve the needs of its customers to the extent that they want to come back again and again and pay for that experience. The target of Christina's mission and its sources of revenue are one in the same.

"Now, back to the homeless shelter. Who is the homeless shelter trying to serve—who is its primary customer? Homeless women, men, and children, right?" Alan nodded. "But who provides the funding for the mission? To be sure, it's not the homeless." Alan again nodded.

"So, the homeless shelter, just like all nonprofits, has two separate sets of customers: one the nonprofit mission is intended to serve and the other that provides the funding necessary to exist." Gene let that thought sink in.

After a long pause, Alan asked, "I get the concept of homeless people being the primary customers or consumers of the homeless shelter's mission, but are you saying that the donors are also customers of the homeless shelter?"

"Yes, but in a different manner. Hold that thought—we'll come back to it in a few minutes. New question: why do you think donors give?" Gene paused and looked at Alan indicating he wanted him to attempt an answer.

Alan was beginning to realize what a good teacher Gene was. "Okay, give me a second to contemplate the question. I think there are probably many reasons. Some give because they want to do something good, make positive change. Some give to be recognized. Am I warm?"

Gene smiled, "Yes. More than warm. The point is every donor gives for some reason, and you came up with two good ones. There are countless more. If every donor gives for a reason, then every donor is seeking something through his or her giving. In other words, a donor's life is enriched in some way through the act of giving. Accepting this basic premise, it stands to reason that serving a donor's passions and interests could lead to greater donor satisfaction and, consequently, greater giving.

"Now, back to your question—yes, donors are a second group of customers and a completely different group of people than the nonprofit mission's primary customers. And they—the donors that is—have needs. Therefore, it is incumbent on nonprofit leadership to understand and serve the donors' needs if they expect giving to continue and grow in the future."

Alan stopped on his crutches and waited for Gene to stop and turn toward him. As soon as Gene made eye contact, Alan put his hands on his head and pulled them away while making an explosion sound. "Gene, my mind is blown."

Gene grinned back at Alan and let the concept settle in for the next few minutes before wrapping up the lesson. As their walk came to an end, Gene said, "So, one final question for you to think about, and I don't want an answer from you today. I want you to think about this question over the next week, and we will discuss it when we meet again. Are you ready for it?"

Alan nodded affirmatively.

"Who within a nonprofit organization should be aware of, think about, and be responsible for serving the needs of this second group of customers, the donors?"

July 6, 7:00 p.m., Red River, New Mexico

Later that evening Alan and Carol were seated on the deck around their firepit and enjoying a glass of wine. Carol thought that Alan seemed preoccupied earlier and decided to be patient with getting the debrief on his meeting with Gene. Now seemed like the right time, so she asked, "Well, how did it go with Gene today? I watched you two walk around the trout pond from our family room window, and it looked like you were having a deep conversation."

After a moment or two of silence, Alan began. "It went nothing like I had planned and couldn't have gone better," and then he looked up at Carol and smiled. "Gene is going to be my consultant for the next few months. You know, honestly, I never really understood why any organization would pay a fundraising consultant. I always assumed fundraising was pretty simple. Gene sure earned his fee today."

Carol jumped in. "Are you paying Gene?"

"No, but I would, knowing now what he can teach me."

Carol asked, "Doesn't Gene have a full-time job? How will he have time to help you?"

"I said the same thing to him. He offered to meet with me once a week through the fall months as long as we can meet early in the morning. There are several key concepts he wants me to learn, the first of which he covered with me today," answered Alan.

"What happens after the next few months?"

"He said we will cross that bridge when we get there.

"The Bensons are leaving tomorrow to head back to McKinney, so we agreed to meet next Monday morning at 6:00 a.m. over coffee. I can't wait. He did give me some homework that will require a listening ear from you. He told me I needed to present to you the lesson he taught me today. Are you up for it?" asked Alan.

"Of course; lay it on me."

From his shirt pocket Alan pulled a piece of paper on which he had outlined Gene's lesson. and he walked Carol thoughtfully through it.

- All nonprofit organizations desire to sustain and grow their missions.
- Sustainability and growth require funding.
- Therefore, every nonprofit organization wants and needs to raise more money.
- And, therefore, every executive director, head of school, or president of a nonprofit must become an effective fundraiser.
- All nonprofit organizations have two equal sets of customers—a huge distinction from for-profit companies.
- The first set is the obvious one and is addressed clearly in the nonprofit's mission statement. It's the reason the nonprofit exists.
- The second set of customers is the source of funding or donors—and is frequently overlooked by nonprofit leadership.
- For a nonprofit organization to thrive, the second group must be acknowledged, embraced, and served with the same care and conviction as the first set of customers.

A half hour later, Alan returned the sheet of paper to his shirt pocket and looked at Carol. "Well, what do you think?"

Carol responded, "I think you have found a very wise friend in Gene. The concept you presented is so simple and common-sense based, yet completely different from the way we have always thought of fundraising at Lakeview Christian."

"My thoughts precisely," said Alan.

Carol said teasingly, "We have one more day here before we head back. What will you do without your new playmate Gene to entertain you?"

Alan chuckled, indicating the same thought had crossed his mind. "Well, in addition to presenting Gene's lesson to you, I have two more things to accomplish before we head back. The first is fun—I need to answer a question Gene asked me to think about for our next meeting. The second I am dreading—I need to come up with some budget cuts that I will present to the board in a few weeks," Alan said with a frown.

July 7, 5:30 a.m., Red River, New Mexico

Alan emerged from the bedroom with a single crutch and made his way to the coffee pot. He settled into the couch and placed his right leg on the coffee table. It was raining this morning, so it seemed darker than usual. The family of deer didn't make their usual appearance either.

What a trip this had been. Alan and Carol missed their children so much. But this visit opened up a new adventure and reason for being here in the mountains. After some deep thought and prayer time, Alan picked up his iPad and reviewed the budget projections in search of areas to make cuts.

Before he realized it, two hours had passed. Alan had a list of cuts that represented cost savings of $75,000. In addition, refinancing the long-term debt would save another $30,000. That still left a couple hundred thousand dollars of deficit spending that Lakeview Christian could not withstand.

Alan laid his iPad aside and gazed out the window again. *That's it*, he thought. *The rest will have to come from fundraising.* He made a mental note to add that to the agenda for his meeting with Gene next week.

With the painful task out of the way, Alan now let his mind focus on Gene's question. *Who within a nonprofit organization should be responsible for serving the donors?*

It occurred to Alan that no one at Lakeview Christian thinks about donors today. But what about other organizations to which he and Carol contribute?

Both Alan and Carol give to their alma maters. Alan graduated from a small liberal arts school in the Midwest and Carol from a large university in Texas. They receive phone calls, emails, and direct mail regularly from both institutions. Alan quickly concluded that development staff is the answer to Gene's question. They are the ones who wake up every day and come to work thinking about the donors, Alan affirmed in his mind.

Alan continued the thought. *Maybe this is Gene's way of telling me that LCA needs to have a development director, someone who only thinks about potential sources of funding.* With that thought, Alan got up to refill his coffee and get on with the day.

July 7, 6:30 p.m., Texas Reds restaurant, Red River, New Mexico

Carol convinced Alan—crutches and all—to take her out to dinner on their last evening in Red River. With live music in the background and a great steak in front of him, Alan was feeling happy. Tyler and Amy FaceTimed them that afternoon and shared how much they missed being there this year and promised to try for next year.

Alan and Carol reminisced about the week behind them, laughing about the way Gene and Karen came into their lives. Both were looking forward to continuing their new friendships back home in McKinney.

Then Carol asked, "Did you make any progress today on your outstanding tasks?"

Alan responded, "Why, yes, I did. I managed to trim a little here and there on the budget and find some cost savings. But the rest will have to come from adding revenue from fundraising. And I am not looking forward to that conversation will Bill."

Carol smiled. "If you present an argument to Bill as convincing as you did with me last night, Bill will get it."

"I hope you're right. Still not looking forward to it," he said, grinning.

"How about the other task?" asked Carol.

"Gene asked me to think about who within a nonprofit organization should be responsible for serving the needs of the donors—aka, the second set of customers. I think he is nudging me to conclude that we need a development director. After all, that is the one department that specifically does what Gene is asking about."

"Hmm, that makes sense. But what about you?"

Alan looked back at Carol somewhat startled. "What do you mean, *me*?"

"I mean, shouldn't you also be responsible for the second set of customers? If you were the president of a manufacturing company, wouldn't you have responsibility for both manufacturing and sales?"

Alan suddenly felt embarrassed for not realizing this. "You're absolutely right. Wow! Now you are teaching me about fundraising."

July 8, 1:36 p.m., Highway 287 in Central Texas

Having left Red River earlier that morning, Alan and Carol were only a few hours away from their home in McKinney, Texas. While they normally split up the drive into two-hour shifts, Carol had to drive the entire way due to Alan's right ankle being in a boot.

"You doing okay, honey? Sorry I'm not much help today," offered Alan.

"I'm good. You can make it up to me with a shoulder rub tonight," said Carol.

"I've been thinking about our conversation last night over dinner and how you helped me find a better answer to Gene's question. Maybe there is still more to it."

"What are you thinking?" asked Carol.

"Well, if we agree that it is my job as headmaster to think about the needs of both sets of customers, wouldn't that also fall within the board's responsibilities? After all, revenue equals mission. And our revenue will come from a combination of tuition and fundraising.

How can the board not own our approach to both sets of customers?"

"I see your point," affirmed Carol. "So the list is growing. Maybe this is exactly what Gene had in mind when he asked you not to answer until you meet next week."

PART III

While there is perhaps a province in which the photograph can tell us nothing more than what we see with our own eyes, there is another in which it proves to us how little our eyes permit us to see.
— Dorothea Lange

Monday, July 10, 5:45 a.m., Lakeview Christian Academy, McKinney, Texas

Alan arrived early to make coffee and set out bagels in anticipation of his meeting with Gene. They had talked briefly by phone over the weekend to confirm the meeting, and Alan was both eager and nervous because it was the first time to meet in McKinney, away from Alan's sanctuary in Red River.

At 5:56 a.m., Gene walked to the front doors of Lakeview Christian. Alan greeted him with a warm handshake. "Welcome to Lakeview Christian Academy, Gene!"

"Hi, Alan! Great to see you. No crutches! How's it going?"

Alan looked down at his boot-clad ankle. "Well, I'm not entirely free of the crutches. I still need them for stairs and longer distances."

"Great news," affirmed Gene. "You know, I have driven past LCA dozens of times and never imagined I would have a reason to visit. Show me around."

After a brief tour of the school, the two men settled in Alan's office around his small conference table. "Wow! Breakfast and everything," teased Gene.

"It is the least I can do and pales in comparison to what you are doing to help me," offered Alan.

After a brief word of prayer, fixing bagels, and catching up on happenings since returning from Red River, their conversation transitioned into the matters at hand. Alan led off. "I want you to know I completed my homework assignments."

Gene smiled, "Great! Did you win over Carol with the first concept?"

"As a matter of fact, I did. She has been a great sounding board and source of encouragement."

"Glad to hear it. How about the other assignment?" asked Gene.

"Yes, I have completed that assignment as well, several times actually," answered Alan with a grin. "The more I think about it, my answer keeps changing."

Gene smiled big while nodding affirmation, "Do tell!"

"I first thought you were indirectly suggesting that I needed to hire a development director—you know, someone who is dedicated to thinking about the second set of customers, the donors. Then my wife hit me between the eyes over dinner at Texas Reds with the notion that the donors' needs should also be my responsibility."

Gene continued to nod and smile. "You married well."

Alan continued, "Then during the drive home, I surmised that if it were my responsibility, then the board should *also* own both sets of customers. So, there it is. My answer is the board, me, and a future development director."

"Not bad at all. You got most of the way there. I'm proud of you, Alan," offered Gene.

Alan's face immediately showed concern, "What do you mean, *most of the way there*? Do you mean there is more?"

"I think, given a few more days, you would have gotten to the full answer, which is everyone at Lakeview Christian."

"Do you mean everyone as in the faculty and staff?"

"Yup!" confirmed Gene. "You are coming to realize that you have two equal and codependent missions. Both missions must be embraced by everyone who is part of the school. You should expect the math teacher to support the mission to donors just as you will expect a development director in the future to support the educational mission."

Alan once again did the mind exploding gesture with his hands. "Wow! I get it."

Gene quickly added, "That doesn't mean that the math teacher must become a fundraiser. What it really means is that the math teacher should understand, acknowledge, and embrace both missions. Think about the access that faculty members have to parents. If the math teacher happens to be sitting beside a parent at a school soccer game and the parent asks about why LCA is fundraising, you want the math teacher to be able to explain it. You certainly wouldn't want the opposite—for the teacher to raise his hands saying he has no idea because he is really not in the loop on these things."

"I see your point and agree. We are all on both teams and support both missions," affirmed Alan. "But what is the second mission really?"

"That is exactly the right question to be asking and one for you and the board to address. Right now, you have a vision and mission for Lakeview Christian that only addresses your mission to students. A key step to engaging the board is to have them craft and adopt a separate mission statement for the second set of customers."

Alan nodded while sitting back in his chair. It all made perfect sense. If both missions are equal and codependent, then the board should own both. Alan offered, "I have some work to do with the board. We have a meeting in two weeks, and I think this should be a key objective."

Gene agreed to help Alan think through the action steps necessary to prepare for the board meeting.

"Now," Gene moved on, "let's start attacking your short-term challenge. How much do you think LCA needs to raise this year to balance the budget?"

Alan was ready for this one. "By my figures, we need at least an additional $200,000 in the next 11 months in order to avoid using the small amount remaining in reserves. Is that what you are expecting... or is this a lost cause?" he added hopefully.

"WHAT!!" Gene shouted in shock. Upon seeing Alan's startled reaction, he quickly added, "Yeah, that's about what I expected." They had a hearty laugh, and then Gene continued.

"Okay, we are going to attempt to solve the short-term challenge by Christmas, leaving you January through June next year to address the long-term challenge," announced Gene.

"Okay, that sounds optimistic," said Alan. "I'm putty in your hands, consultant Benson. Let's get started. Are we going to plan an event?"

"Believe it or not, events will have nothing to do with addressing the short-term challenge. Events are labor intensive, expensive, and bring too little return for what you need. You will incorporate an event strategy to address the long-term challenge, but our focus will be on 20 to 25 people to address the short-term challenge." Gene delivered that last line while watching Alan closely. He could see a concerned look growing on his face.

After about 30 seconds of silence, Alan asked, "So what you're saying is that we are going to get 20 people to give about $10,000 each, right? Gene, we don't have that many donors who can give gifts that size. We have never received gifts like that before. I'm worried you might have a misunderstanding of our constituency."

After another brief pause, Gene responded in a calming tone of voice. "Alan, you are right that I really don't know your constituency. I am still getting to know Lakeview Christian. But I'm going to say something that might sound bold to you, even arrogant. So just hang in here with me." Alan nodded cautiously while Gene proceeded. "You do have constituents with the capacity to give significant gifts, probably well in excess of what you need this year.

You just don't realize it because you have never engaged them in a way that produces such gifts."

The two men stared at each other for a solid minute while Alan prepared to respond. Finally, he broke the silence. "Gene, I just don't see it. The expression, 'you can't squeeze blood from a turnip' comes to mind."

That last statement brought a smile to Gene's face. "First of all, we are not looking for blood, and the people who love Lakeview Christian are not turnips. And your reaction to this concept is normal, so again, please hang with me a little longer." Alan nodded.

Gene continued, "I want to share a story with you that may change your perspective on this issue. Here it is:

> *Imagine that Carol and you join Karen and me at an event for a cause you feel strongly about. You have probably been to events like the one I will describe. We arrive at a large hotel and make our way toward the ballrooms. We stop to check in at a table where we receive our nametags and table assignments—let's say it's table number 37.*
>
> *As we walk into the ballroom, we are taken for a moment by its size and decor. There are probably 50 or more tables set for dinner with beautiful floral centerpieces. We eventually locate table 37 and take our seats where we enjoy small talk and meet the others seated at our table.*

A few minutes later someone takes the podium and explains the activities of the evening. After we complete our meals, others speak and tell a compelling story about the cause we are all there to support. Then we watch a video about this mission that brings tears to our eyes.

Finally, a couple at our table stands up and introduces themselves as our table captains. They distribute packets and invite each of us to make a gift in support of this cause.

Let's say that the Bensons and the Morgans each decide to give $1,000 to the cause. Now you might give more or less than that, but for the sake of my story, we each give $1,000. We complete a pledge card allowing us to pay the gift over several months.

Gene paused the story and said, "Here's a question for you, Alan. What would you expect in return for such a gift?"

Alan thought a moment and then responded, "I would expect to be thanked. And I would expect a receipt at some point for tax purposes."

Gene nodded. "Those are reasonable expectations. Maybe you would even get a handwritten note from the table captains. But we probably wouldn't expect much more. Let me continue the story."

The day following the event, the four of us are walking down a street in Dallas on our way to a restaurant for dinner, and we pass a homeless man seated and holding a sign asking for help. This is an experience we have all had many times. Full disclosure here, you know what my job is at Collin County Family Services, and sometimes I walk past and try not to make eye contact. But other times I might stop and give the homeless man a five- or ten-dollar bill, say, "God bless you. Get a hot meal," and then walk on.

Alan nodded, indicating he might do the same.

"Next question, Alan. Why wouldn't we give the homeless man a thousand dollars?" Gene let that question hang for several seconds watching Alan's face and then added, "It sounds a bit crazy right? But according to my story, last night we went to that event and gave a thousand dollars. The homeless man's needs are probably well beyond a thousand dollars. What keeps us from giving that much to the homeless man?"

A small grin grew on Alan's face as he contemplated the question. Gene once again jumped in to break the long silence. "There are some good reasons that prevent us from giving that much to the homeless man. We might be putting him at risk for having that much money and someone else might mug him in an alley because he wants it more. We might be perpetuating a drug or alcohol habit that we are unaware of. Lots of things keep us from giving like that."

Alan nodded, grateful that Gene helped him with an answer.

Gene continued, "There is one more brief component to the story."

The next day, day three, you are walking down the same street in Dallas and pass the same homeless man. As you are recognizing him, he waves at you and says thank you for the five bucks you gave him yesterday. And then he asks you if you would be willing to talk with him over a cup of coffee at the coffee shop you are standing in front of.

Over that cup of coffee, he says to you, "If you would be willing to invest a thousand dollars in me, I will transform my life over the next 90 days. I will do this, this, and this (defining the steps he plans to take). And you can give it to me in small pieces. I will meet you here at this coffee shop every Tuesday at 2:00 p.m. and report to you my progress. And if ever I don't do what I promised, you can stop supporting me."

"Next question, would you do it?"

Alan had a larger grin on his face, and he began to nod. Gene went on, "I would, too. And the homeless man would likely get more than a thousand. What just happened here? A minute ago the idea of giving a thousand dollars to the homeless man was preposterous. And now it is probable."

Alan was still smiling somewhat in disbelief of the journey Gene took him on with the story. "That is an incredible illustration, Gene."

Gene wrapped up the lesson by explaining the concept of *transformational giving*. "You see, Alan, most people are familiar with *transactional giving*. That is the kind of giving we do when we reach in our pockets and hand over a five-dollar bill or when we respond to direct mail or digital requests for gifts. Even most event fundraising is transactional in nature. But transformational giving happens when we are engaged in the mission, when we know exactly how our gift will create positive change, and when there is accountability. That's what the homeless man did with you over coffee. And giving like that is not only transformational for the recipient, it is also transformational for the donor."

"Once again, Gene, you have completely blown up my understanding of giving."

"Now, Alan, we are going to talk through the actions we need to take, and there will be homework to be done every week for the next few months. Are you prepared to make this your priority?"

"I am. I have no choice."

"Are you prepared to fight some battles with your board?" continued Gene.

"I think so. What kinds of battles?"

"Nothing crazy. We will take one step at a time, and perhaps we won't incur that many battles, but I just want to warn you that our plan can't happen in a vacuum. It will require the support of others in leadership, and there will be some pushback along the way," explained Gene.

Alan was now realizing that they were about to change the culture of LCA. And this change was both good and necessary. But, as Gene pointed out, change never happens without resistance.

Gene walked Alan through the tasks that would lay the foundation for addressing the short-term challenge of raising $200,000. Alan quickly learned that Gene wasn't kidding about a time commitment, at least for the next few months. But Alan had no idea how right Gene was about the battles he would have to fight.

July 10, 5:15 p.m., the Morgans' home

Alan couldn't wait to present to Carol his lesson from Gene that morning. Alan had spent most of the day getting a jump on some of the work Gene had assigned, but his favorite part of the homework was to re-teach Gene's lesson. Although Carol was a full-time faculty member at LCA, she was enjoying the month of July at home, a perk for most in the teaching profession.

Alan hobbled in the door, boot and all, with extra spring in his step. "Hi, Carol. I'm home." Alan left his briefcase in the entry and made his way back to the kitchen to grab a soft drink from the fridge. He spotted Carol through the kitchen window in the backyard.

Carol had been working in their vegetable garden most of the afternoon and was feeling a bit weary from the heat. Her knees were sore, and she had managed to smudge dirt on a few areas of her face. She looked up as she heard Alan open the back door and limp to a chair on the patio. "Hi, honey. I'm just finishing up. I'll be with you in a few."

Alan waved and told her to take her time. He sat back and took in the view. Not quite the view he had in Red River, but it was peaceful. The Morgans' home backed up to a wooded area, so they saw quite a few deer and other wildlife. Carol kept the yard in flowers most of the year, and it always looked beautiful.

Minutes later, Carol approached Alan from the yard. "How was your day today, Dr. Morgan?" she asked knowing full well that he had met with Gene this morning.

"Once again, Gene didn't disappoint. I can't wait to tell you all about it."

Before Carol excused herself to clean up, she informed Alan that there was a lasagna in the oven that would soon burn and that he should get it out now while she showered. "Okay, okay, I got it. See you in a while."

As Carol walked inside, Alan relaxed and thought back to Red River. He thought of the family of deer he saw most mornings across the trout pond. *Probably not the same family and silly of me to think so. How peaceful they looked though.* He was sometimes envious of them, not carrying the burdens in life that humans did. *How nice it might be to have no big worries.* Alan allowed his thoughts to drift to Tyler and Amy. He wondered what they were doing this very minute—probably *not* thinking about their parents. Although they were now young adults and caring for themselves, he and Carol still constantly worried about them. That worry will probably never go away.

Suddenly the back door sprung open and Carol emerged with a towel wrapped around her hair. "Alan!" she shouted, yanking him out of his deep state of thought. "The lasagna!"

Alan jumped to his feet, forgetting the boot on his right ankle and winced in pain as he stood up. "I'm sorry, Carol," he called back and hobbled toward the house. By the time he was inside, Carol was already pulling their burned dinner out of the oven. Alan realized he screwed up and needed to make this right. "I am so sorry, honey. I got lost in a daydream and forgot."

Carol was clearly miffed and disappointed that her work that afternoon making the lasagna was now wasted. "It's alright. I can make some sandwiches instead."

"This is all my fault, and I want to make it up to you. Let's go out to dinner. I'll clean up this mess while you get ready." Alan put his arms around Carol and kissed her forehead. "Thank you for making the lasagna. I do love your lasagna. Please let me make this right."

Carol reluctantly agreed and headed back to their bedroom to get ready.

As Alan scraped the burned lasagna into the garbage can in the garage, he thought of an idea. He limped back to the kitchen and finished cleaning up when Carol reemerged looking ready to go out. She said, "I guess I can forgive you if you take me someplace nice."

"Deal!" said Alan, "But I want to make a stop on the way."

They jumped in the car and headed toward the east side of McKinney. Although Alan wouldn't say, Carol had an idea where they might be going. "Are we going to see Gene by chance?"

"Sort of," Alan confessed. "We are stopping by his agency, Collin County Family Services. I have been curious about it since meeting Gene in Red River. Let's just check it out."

McKinney is one of the fastest-growing small cities in America for the past decade and is now home to nearly 200,000 people. Alan surmised that, with rapid growth, all segments of the population grow and that includes the segment in poverty. The east side is where poverty is most evident, and this is precisely why CCFS is located here. Alan hadn't really spent much time on this side of town and was not sure exactly where CCFS was.

"Alan, seeing this part of town makes me sad. We should do more to help," said Carol.

At last they drove in front of a large, red-brick building that looked newer than most of the buildings in the area. Above the door was a backlit sign that indicated they had arrived. Alan pulled into a parking place, and the Morgans walked up the paved path and through the front doors.

The lobby was tastefully decorated and had lots of seating. There was also a play area for small children. There were only a couple of people seated in the lobby, but Alan deduced that was due to the time of day. It was already 6:40 p.m.

Alan walked up to the reception counter and was immediately greeted by the woman behind the counter. "Hi there, I'm Cindy. How can I help you today?"

Alan was impressed. "Hi, I'm Alan, and this is my wife, Carol. We are friends of Gene Benson."

"Okay, great. I think he is still here. Is he expecting you?" asked Cindy.

"Not really, but can you check?"

Less than a minute later, Gene emerged, "Alan, Carol—what a surprise!"

"I know, Gene. We're sorry for dropping in on you like this. Carol and I are on our way to get some late dinner and thought we would drive by Collin County Family Services since neither of us have been here. We actually thought you would already be gone for the day."

"No worries at all," said Gene. "Believe it or not, Karen is meeting me downtown at 7:15 to have dinner. Would you two care to join us?"

Alan looked at Carol who quickly nodded yes. "Sounds great!"

Gene added, "I have a few more things to take care of before I leave, and Karen won't be at the restaurant for 30 more minutes. Would you like a tour?"

Both said yes and then smiled at each other, as if to say *jinx* through mental telepathy.

"Great! You probably met Cindy when you walked in. Cindy, would you mind giving my friends a tour while I finish up?" She readily agreed.

Cindy was a fantastic tour guide and really understood the mission. She explained to the Morgans how families are referred and what kinds of life challenges most families face. They learned about the continuum of services available, from help paying utilities to job training, to family medical and dental care, and even some transitional housing for families to get back on their feet.

After 10 minutes or so, Alan asked Cindy how long she had been a receptionist for CCFS. Cindy replied politely and respectfully, "I'm not a staff member. I'm actually a client and volunteer." Suddenly Alan felt embarrassed, and Cindy sensed it. "It's okay. I'm flattered by your question. I first came to CCFS a few years after my husband left me. Gene and the staff here at CCFS have been terrific and helped me through the toughest time of my life. So now I volunteer here two evenings a week."

"Wow, what a great story," Carol chimed in. "I'm so happy for you, Cindy!"

"Thank you. I love this place. I see people walk in here all the time with similar challenges. I love that I can be a part of it as a volunteer," said Cindy.

The next stop on the tour was an introduction to a social worker who counsels clients through the various services and programs offered by CCFS. "Hello, I'm Walter."

They all shook hands, and then Alan spoke up, "Walter, this might seem like a crazy question, but I'm going to ask it anyway. Who do you serve here at CCFS? Who is your customer?"

Walter smiled broadly and confidently began his answer. "We serve many people, but I would put them into two broad groups. The first group consists of the people who are in need of our services, whether they are just going through a tough streak in life or whether their problems are deeper. The second would be the ones who fund our mission. Without them, none of the first group could be served."

Alan couldn't believe it. Neither could Carol, who leaned over and whispered into Alan's ear, "I wonder how many faculty and staff at LCA would give that answer."

The final stop on the tour was Gene's office. It was a humble office but well organized. A framed photograph immediately caught Alan's eye. "Was that taken in Red River by chance?"

"Right you are!" answered Gene proudly. "When things get stressful around here, I will close my door and take a few minutes to lose myself in that photograph. It's almost like being transported back to the mountains and feeling that sense of peace."

July 10, 7:45 p.m., Local Yocal restaurant, McKinney, Texas

Over dinner the Bensons and Morgans picked up right where they left off in Red River. They were all comfortable together—it never felt like work to find something to talk about.

Alan decided to report back to Gene on his little test during their tour of CCFS. "Gene, I must confess that I conducted an experiment today with Walter, the social worker."

Gene's eyebrows raised in curiosity. "What did you do?"

"I asked him who CCFS's customer was. And I'll be danged if he didn't say exactly what you taught me the other day." They all had a good chuckle. "I am so impressed that someone who is so ingrained in the core mission of CCFS is so aware of the funding side. Walter even told us that, on occasion, he leads donor tours for the development staff. Why Walter?"

Gene finished chewing his bite of steak and then looked up at Alan, "Who better to explain our mission than someone who lives it firsthand every day?"

"So, everything must run perfect at CCFS under your leadership," added Alan.

That immediately drew belly laughs from both Gene and Karen. It was Karen who spoke first. "As good a fundraiser as Gene is, he has plenty of dysfunction going on at CCFS. Trust me, I hear about it all the time." Gene nodded in agreement with Karen's statement while he chewed another bite of steak.

"What kinds of dysfunction could you possibly have?" asked Alan skeptically.

"Well, for one, my board is a perpetual challenge. They don't quite understand the difference between governance and management. I am working very hard right now to get the board out of the weeds."

The four friends continued to talk about their families and other things over dessert and coffee. The restaurant manager finally approached the table and asked how much longer they planned to stay, Not realizing it was now 10:30 p.m. and the doors had been locked for the last 30 minutes, they got up apologizing, exchanged hugs, and said goodnight.

On the way home, Alan told the homeless man story to Carol. She agreed that the story was a powerful illustration for giving.

Over the next few days, Alan took advantage of the peace and quiet at LCA while faculty enjoyed time off and dove into his assigned tasks that he and Gene discussed. He had three:

1. Prepare a copy of the LCA annual budget that showed everything except faculty and staff salaries. Alan didn't yet understand why Gene wanted this but decided to accept the task because it was the easiest of the three.

2. Outline the LCA story, explaining why the school needs to raise money. This was a challenging task because the answer really can't be, "So we can pay our bills."

3. Identify 10 families that may have capacity to give. This list could include grandparents of students, alumni parents, or current parents.

The budget was done. Alan had already printed two copies and laid them aside for his meeting with Gene next Monday morning. Alan immediately observed that there wasn't much of a budget when you remove the faculty and staff salaries. LCA's staff account for over 80 percent of the school's $5 million budget.

Alan glanced down the list of items within the remainder of the budget. There were scholarships, utilities, supplies for the various academic disciplines, a couple of field trips, building and grounds upkeep, athletics, arts, and a few other smaller line items. *Maybe Gene thinks we should try to shave a little more off to reduce the need for fundraising,* Alan thought.

Alan next skipped to the third task of identifying families with perceived financial capacity. Alan knew that Bill, his board chair, would not approve of this exercise. It did feel awkward—like sizing up the fatted calf before slaughter. Nonetheless, Alan started a list on a legal pad. There were a few families with students at LCA who did very well financially. In fact, there were several who probably didn't even feel the pain of paying tuition. Alan began writing names and realized how quickly he got to 10. He added a few more and then put the legal pad away.

On to the story task. Alan concluded he needed his elevator speech, and the best way to do that was to say it out loud. There was no one else in the building, so why not?

"Lakeview Christian Academy has been providing a Christ-centered education with a Kingdom worldview to McKinney-area students for the past 15 years. Our goal is to continue to provide the highest-quality education possible. And for this reason, LCA needs your financial support."

Wow! Did that ever sound boring, Alan thought. Alan tried it a few more times but kept thinking he sounded like an uninteresting brochure.

Suddenly Alan heard some racket just outside his open office door. "Hello?" he called out.

"Hi, Dr. Morgan. It's me, Earl. I'm just emptying the wastebaskets in here. I'm sorry if I disturbed you."

Earl was the school custodian and probably the only other LCA employee working today. Alan got up from his desk chair and came out to greet him.

"Hi, Earl. How are you?" asked Alan as he extended his hand. "How's your summer?"

"Pretty quiet around here over the summer. I was surprised when I heard voices coming from your office. I'm usually the only one here most of July. Are you meeting with a new family?" asked Earl.

Alan chuckled with embarrassment. "No, no. I was actually practicing telling the LCA story. You caught me talking to myself."

Earl chuckled with Alan and offered, "I understand. Sometimes I sing out loud around here in the summer. You wouldn't want to hear that."

"Earl," Alan persisted, "can I ask you a question?"

"Sure."

"You have been around here almost as long as I have. What do you think is special about Lakeview Christian?"

Earl gazed up at the corner of the room as he thought about the question. "Lakeview Christian is an amazing place. I see the lives of kids transformed here every day. It's not just the quality education they receive; they become aware of the world around them and how to live in it with reverence and respect for God's creation. I only wish LCA could impact more kids with that experience. The world would be a better place."

"Well said, Earl. Thank you for sharing that with me."

Alan returned to his office, leaned back in his chair, and put his feet up on the desk. He let his mind drift back to Red River, gazing out the front window at the trout pond, mountain, and family of deer. Just thinking of that setting brought calm to Alan. After a few minutes, he replayed Earl's response in his mind. He spoke so naturally about LCA—not rehearsed. And the one line of Earl's that stuck out to Alan was his view that the world would be a better place if more kids could come to LCA.

Why can't more kids come to LCA? Alan contemplated. *What is preventing this from happening?*

It's the high cost associated with educating a student. Tuition rises every year to try to keep pace with the rising costs, and one by one, families are surrendering and leaving, not being able to keep pace with the increases. Although there was some tuition assistance available, most families did not want to go through the process of applying for support provided by other families' tuition.

July 17, 5:45 a.m., Lakeview Christian Academy

With coffee, bagels, and his briefcase monopolizing his hands, Alan opened his office door using his elbow. Gene would be here in 15 minutes, and Alan was excited. He had worked hard this past week on the homework Gene had assigned. And he was excited to show Gene his matching shoes. Today was the first day without the boot.

At 5:59 a.m., Gene greeted Alan at the front doors of LCA. Gene was carrying a large, rectangular, flat object wrapped in brown paper. After shaking hands with Gene, Alan stepped back and bowed with both hands reaching toward his feet. "Well, go figure! You do have matching shoes. The ankle must be feeling better," observed Gene.

"It's still a little stiff, but the doc says I don't need the boot anymore. What's in the package?"

"You'll see," said Gene with a grin.

The two men settled in around the conference table and shared a word of prayer before diving into the bagels and coffee. They caught up on pleasantries for the next few minutes and then cleared the napkins and bagel crumbs in order to get down to business.

"Do you have your homework done?" Gene asked immediately.

"Man, you don't mess around. As a matter of fact, I do. Where should we start?"

"Tell me your story."

Alan was hoping to push this part of the homework to the end. Regardless, he walked through the story he had prepared, building in some of what Earl, the custodian, had shared. When he finished, he looked at Gene for a reaction.

Gene began, "Alan, think about the creative writing classes that are taught here. When you write a story, what are the elements that comprise it?"

Alan immediately rattled off, "Characters, setting, plot, conflict, and resolution. Some things you just never forget."

"What would you say is the most important element to make the story interesting?"

"Well, one could make an argument for any one of the five, but I would say it is the conflict. Without conflict, the story is boring," observed Alan.

"Now, think back to your story. Where is the conflict?"

Alan felt embarrassed that he didn't see that coming. "Oops."

"Why don't we move on to another task for a bit and then come back to the story."

Gene asked to see the budget next. Alan placed the two copies he had prepared in front of them. "As you can see, there isn't much of a budget once people costs are removed."

Gene handed Alan a red felt-tipped marker. "Alan, I want you to circle $200,000 worth of items that you would cut if you had to."

Alan looked at Gene confused. "I thought we were going to raise the $200,000?"

"We are. Just hang with me for a few minutes, and let's work through this exercise. For instance, you can't really cut utilities or building and grounds maintenance. But you could cut the football budget if you had to, right?"

"Only if I want to incite a riot! This is Texas, Gene!"

Gene explained, "Relax, Alan. I'm not suggesting you should cut football, but LCA is a school first and foremost. Athletics and arts are vital to any school, but not more important than core academics, teachers, and classroom space in which to learn. Circle the athletics and arts items, and let's keep searching."

Alan proceeded under protest, arguing every time Gene asked him to circle an item. They eventually circled enough items that represented $200,000.

"That was painful, wasn't it?" asked Gene.

"There is nothing left except a foundation, walls, and a roof. We would lose all of our students," cried Alan.

"Exactly. All those items circled in red represent your margin of excellence. Without those items, you have the bare bones of a school. With those items, you have an awesome educational experience."

Suddenly the lights in Alan's head came on. "I think I see where you are going. We need to raise $200,000 to pay for this stuff because this stuff represents the margin between mediocrity and excellence." And now more lights. "And that's the conflict in my story!"

Gene reached across and fist-bumped Alan. "Now how about the last task?"

Alan pulled the legal pad from his desk drawer and showed the list to Gene. Gene complimented his work and agreed with the reasons that Alan offered for including each name. Gene then assigned homework for the coming week.

"That is all I have for our meeting, but we still have some time. What questions do you have about this process?" asked Gene.

"One thing that has been on my mind is my board. I have a board meeting coming up in 10 days and am wondering how and when I let them know that LCA is working with a consultant and how best to introduce you to them."

"Whoa! Slow down there. LCA is not working with a consultant. And your board will likely take your head off if they think you hired a consultant without their involvement and blessing. They may not even believe LCA needs a consultant," explained Gene. "I am your consultant—but really more of an advisor. You will need to be the mouthpiece to the board until the board is ready and willing to take outside counsel. In the meantime, you need to completely own the ideas you want the board to embrace."

Alan looked disappointed. "I was kind of hoping you might come and present to the board some of the concepts you have presented to me. You are so eloquent the way you teach and have the experience to back it up."

"There will come a time when you will need an outside voice to speak to your board—someone who can effect necessary change," offered Gene. "I wouldn't have managed the past seven years without some help."

Alan was stunned. "You use consultants? Why would *you* need a consultant? You used to do this and already know what to do."

Gene chuckled. "I need a consultant just as much as you do. It's not about what I know; it is the outside perspective, the discipline, and insistent voice that represents the true value of a consultant. But let's get back to the challenge at hand."

Gene spent the next few minutes explaining to Alan how he needed to be viewed as the instigator of these ideas. And while there would be a time and place to consider an outside consultant to be a strong voice to the board, Alan would need to fight and win the battles if any significant change was to be made in the immediate future. Gene concluded with adding an additional task to that week's homework assignment. He asked Alan to spend some time thinking through the possible objections that the board will raise to the concepts Alan will eventually present.

"One last thing before I leave. I brought you a gift." Gene handed Alan the brown-paper-wrapped package.

Alan removed the brown paper with care. It was a large framed photograph of Alan's favorite view through the front window in Red River. He was speechless. "How did you know?"

"I saw how you looked at the photograph in my office the other day. I asked Carol what your happy place is, and she told me it was gazing out across the pond at the mountain from the couch in Red River. So, I asked a friend of mine who lives in Red River to make this photograph. I hope this will help you with your thinking in the months ahead."

Alan embraced Gene with a man hug and said thank you.

July 20, 7:30 a.m., Lakeview Christian School

Alan reclined in his desk chair, feet on his desk, and coffee cup in hand as he stared at the photograph Gene gave to him. It was now mounted on his office wall opposite his desk. What an incredibly thoughtful gift. He took it home Monday to show Carol, and it was her idea that he place it in his office. Alan was in his happy place.

He was headlong into his homework and was now in deep thought about the board. Alan already completed the other tasks Gene had assigned. There were two, not including the task about the board's potential questions:

1. Go back over the list of families with perceived capacity to give that was created the week prior. The task was to identify an area of interest for each. Gene gave him four categories in which to place each family: academics, arts, athletics, or faculty/student support. The purpose of this exercise was to begin to match these families to something for which they have passion.

2. Build a financial model for the $200,000 need. Gene gave him a worksheet that consisted of 20 empty boxes. Alan's task was to place dollar amounts in each of the 20 boxes that total at least $200,000. And Gene stipulated that he couldn't just make all 20 boxes the same value of $10,000 each. He actually wrote in the figure of $40,000 in the top left box, indicating that box was not optional.

Now he allowed his mind to drift back into the boardroom. What will they say? What questions will they ask? What will they object to?

Alan again pulled out his legal pad and began making notes about issues on which he needed board buy in. He then started thinking through the personalities in the room and began listing potential questions and arguments:

- *Why can't we balance the budget with tuition alone? The for-profit world manages.*

- *If we have to raise money, why not just put on an auction like other nonprofits do?*

- *Is it even ethical to ask our tuition-paying families to give more?*

- *Asking for specific gifts feels wrong, like asking people to measure up to our prejudged amounts.*

- *Aren't we just pretending to be friends with these people to get to their money?*

- *What about all the other families? Why are we placing the burden on only a few?*

Wow, Alan thought. *If I'm at all close to the truth here, I have a pretty cynical board. I can't wait to hear how Gene would answer these questions.*

Alan's eyes went back to the photograph. Aside from Carol, he couldn't remember anyone giving him a gift that was so personal.

July 22, 2:00 p.m., at the Morgans' home

Alan and Carol were elated that their kids were home for a brief visit. Tyler and Amy arrived that morning and would return to campus the next afternoon. Both were reluctant to take the break due to the heavy workload of summer session. But they missed their parents and wanted to be home for a couple of days.

Tyler, the older child by 19 months, was finishing up his MBA. He put a lot of pressure on himself to make top grades and had to work hard to meet his own expectations. Amy was the overachiever and was aiming to graduate in just three years by utilizing the summer semesters. Unlike her older brother, near perfect grades came naturally to her without much effort, which drove Ty absolutely crazy.

Alan was on the patio tending to chicken and burgers on the grill when Ty came out to chat.

"I knew about your ankle from Mom's reports, but she was just filling us in on your new friends. Way to go, Dad."

"Well hey, when you two stood us up in Red River, we had to do something with our time," joked Alan. Alan handed the tongs and spatula to his son and took a seat at the patio table. Ty took over without missing a beat. "Are you familiar with Collin County Family Services on the east side of town?" Alan asked.

"Yeah. I did some of my service hours there during high school. They do a lot for our community. It was an interesting experience."

"What do you mean, *interesting*?"

"Well, about halfway through my hours my junior year, the lady who ran the place got fired, and we were told that we would have to complete our service hours elsewhere. I ended up finishing my hours at the McKinney retirement home," explained Tyler.

"Now that you mention it, I have a vague memory of something like that happening. The reason I asked is because Gene Benson, my new friend from Red River," Alan winked at Ty, "is the executive director there now. Gene said he has been there for about seven years, so he must have come shortly after his predecessor was removed."

Over the dinner table, the conversation was mostly about Tyler's and Amy's classes and campus life. Both kids are anxious to finish college and get on with their careers. Amy is interested in the family business of teaching and was already interning as a student aide at a private school near the Baylor campus. Tyler was ready to take on the business world and make his first million by age 25.

As Carol and Amy were in the kitchen slicing the cheesecake and pouring coffee, Ty asked his dad about Lakeview Christian. "Mom also told me you have been mega stressed over the school's finances. Is everything okay?"

"It's not good right now, Ty. We are struggling to balance the books. When you kids were growing up at LCA, we were growing as a school, adding 20 to 30 new kids every year. I have come to learn recently that it is much easier to manage into growing revenue than into shrinking revenue."

Ty nodded in understanding. "In one of my business classes, we are doing case studies on this very thing. If it's any consolation, even big corporations sometimes struggle with that same challenge."

"My new friend Gene is helping me enter into the fundraising realm," said Alan just as Amy and Carol were sitting down.

Carol added, "Gene spent most of his life consulting with nonprofit leaders on fundraising. He has literally turned our understanding of fundraising upside down these past few weeks."

Amy chimed in, "At the school where I'm interning, I got to spend a couple of days with the headmaster. She says she spends nearly half her time raising funds for the school. She also warned me that my college education would not prepare me for that part of the job."

Alan looked up from his dessert. "That's exactly what Gene told me."

Ty weighed in, "It actually makes sense to me that the education path wouldn't necessarily lead to the position of head in any school. Think about any major corporation, like an automobile manufacturer. The CEO probably did not come up through the factory or engineering path and probably doesn't know more about cars than those who work for him or her. The CEO probably came from another industry and simply knows how to run a profitable company. Wouldn't the same be true in the nonprofit world?"

"Ty, that's ridiculous!" scolded Amy. "A head of school should always be an educator. How else could the appropriate educational vision and mission be created and embraced?"

"Hey, I'm just saying, look around and watch what is working," shot back Ty.

Alan and Carol smiled at each other, happy that their chicks were back in the nest and that things seemed beautifully normal as Tyler and Amy argued with each other.

July 24, 5:59 a.m., Lakeview Christian Academy

Gene and Alan greeted each other in the usual manner and place, began with a word of prayer, and dove into bagels and coffee.

"I like the location you chose for the photograph. That is precisely what I had in mind," observed Gene.

"Thanks again. I have had several sessions this past week with my feet on the desk staring at it. The view really does transport me to Red River and gives me peace."

Alan continued, "Our kids, Ty and Amy, were home over the weekend. It was so great to see them. Ty reminded me that he did part of his school service hours at CCFS."

"No kidding! I heard from some of the staff that CCFS used do that with the nearby schools," offered Gene.

"Ty mentioned that his time there was cut short by the departure of the executive director."

"Ah yes," affirmed Gene. "He must have been there about eight years ago then. That is when CCFS went through its scandal." Gene used both hands to make quotation marks when he said the word *scandal*. "That was a rough time for CCFS. My predecessor was the founder of CCFS and had been around a long time. She had few checks and balances and, as it turned out, was embezzling from the agency."

Alan's forehead wrinkled a bit showing concern. "Oh my. Ty said there was a rumor going around that she was fired, but he had no idea why."

"Yes, few people learned the entire story. The board took immediate action and tried their best to keep the embezzlement thing quiet. They did not press charges so long as she agreed to repay what was stolen."

"That was a kind gesture on the part of the board," observed Alan.

"Believe me, their primary motive was to protect the agency from scandal, not to be kind to her. And they were exactly right for acting in that way. That is a key role for a board to play. Unfortunately, though, I inherited a different culture—one where there is little trust."

"Is this what you were eluding to over dinner the other night?" asked Alan.

"Yes," affirmed Gene. "As a result of what happened eight years ago, my board has probably overcorrected and now has its fingers in many things it shouldn't. Enough about my problems. Let's get you ready for your board meeting."

With that, Alan pulled out his legal pad and folder from of his desk and prepared to update Gene on his homework. "Let me start with the more functional tasks. Here is my stab at a financial model." Alan handed the worksheet with boxes on it to Gene. "What do you think?"

Gene could see several numbers scratched out in each box illustrating Alan's thought process in completing the exercise. The final numbers on the worksheet were the following.

$40K

$20K $20K

$15K $15K $15K

$10K $10K $10K $10K

$5K $5K $5K $5K $5K

$2K $2K $2K $2K $2K $2K

"Great job! This is a realistic model. I can see you changed your mind a few times to get here. What did you learn by doing this?"

"Come on now, Gene, you forced my hand a bit by filling in the top box. If not for that, I probably would have come up with something completely different. Do you really think we can find a donor to give forty thousand bucks?"

"Maybe," Gene answered. "It depends on many other factors that we will tackle in the coming weeks. Did you take a stab at identifying interests for your list of high-capacity families?"

Alan briefly talked through each of the families on the list and why he believed they had specific interests. There were a few families that he honestly didn't know about. Gene explained that was normal and there are other things they can do to fill in the missing gaps of information.

Alan next flipped to the page on his legal pad with the list of ornery questions that he predicted might come from the board. "I've got to say, Gene, I am feeling some anxiety about my board meeting on Thursday."

"I understand. What do you think they will ask?"

Alan first stepped Gene through the big concepts that he wanted to present and then began with the first question. "I think Bill, my board chair, will still be stuck on what he sees as the root issue: why can't we balance the budget with tuition alone?"

Gene nodded in understanding and then offered a logical explanation. "There is a threshold for tuition in every private school, and it is different in each school based on the socio-economic circumstances of the school families and the culture of the community. The threshold represents the perceived value of the education provided by that private school. When you try to raise tuition beyond that perceived value or threshold, you experience the law of diminishing returns. What you gain in revenue, you lose from a reduction in enrollment."

Gene continued, "Nearly every private school in America must raise part of its operational budget from charitable giving. And because the tuition threshold varies so dramatically from one school to another, the part of the budget addressed through fundraising varies from as little as five percent to as much as forty percent."

Gene handed Alan a few pages of substantive data supporting his case and encouraged him to use this data as necessary. "What's next?" asked Gene.

"Let's assume I successfully make the case for our need to fundraise. I think the board will immediately gravitate in the direction of an event. How can I head that one off at the pass?"

Gene began again, "This is a big issue to tackle with the board, and I agree that they will probably think events are the answer. This is one of the biggest problems most private schools have with their fundraising efforts. If this happens, you should first express your appreciation for their enthusiasm and suggestions and indicate that there will be a time in the near future when you will want their ideas. My counsel is that you ask the board to let you drive the plans to address the short-term challenge of raising $200,000. You are the CEO, the one they pay to operate the business. That is not an unreasonable request."

Alan thought about Gene's point. He's right, the board should trust Alan to manage the tactics of raising the money, the same as they would expect him to hire a new faculty member or select a new social studies curriculum. But Alan knew they would want to know what he had planned, and that is where he feared the real problems would be.

Alan proceeded to the next question. "Okay, I think I'm with you so far. But there will be questions about what I will be doing to raise the money, and I can't say, 'Sorry, it's a secret.'"

"I agree," Gene said while laughing, "I don't think that would fly. What questions do you think you will have to answer?"

"Some members of my board will question the ethics of asking some people for large amounts and not asking others. They will be concerned with fairness and judging people's capacity to give. And I must admit, I have some of the same concerns, Gene. I will struggle with answering these questions."

Gene smiled and nodded in understanding. "Alan, I know this is hard for you. You met this guy in the middle of a mountain in New Mexico four weeks ago who is now pushing you to do and say things to your board that seem wrong and even crazy."

Alan needed Gene to empathize with him, and Gene read the situation perfectly. "I know you are only trying to help me, Gene, and you are giving me an incredible gift for free. In case I haven't said it enough, thank you."

Gene jumped right back into the matter at hand. "Let's come at this board meeting a bit more strategically. How about you ask for a private meeting with Bill tomorrow and give him a heads-up on your strategy?"

Alan considered Gene's suggestion. "You know, that just might work! Bill can sometimes be a bully in the boardroom, and no one likes to challenge him. Dealing with Bill's tough questions beforehand may diffuse some of the conflict I am fearing will dominate the meeting on Thursday."

"Here is one more idea to ponder," added Gene. "Who is the most credible board member, the one others listen to?"

Alan responded immediately, "Easy—that would be Larry Dolan. He is the CEO of MinTec."

Gene recognized the name from Alan's list of high-capacity families. "Why don't you also meet with Larry before the board meeting?"

"Do you mean along with Bill?"

"No, I mean have lunch with Larry on Wednesday and see if you can win him over as a supporter of your plan. You will know by then what Bill's concerns are and can prep Larry to help counter them."

Alan smiled broadly, "Now that is a great idea. I'll do it. But can you still help me address these ethical issues about fundraising?"

Gene laughed and proceeded to tackle each of the concerns Alan raised earlier with logical and credible explanations. Alan took notes feverishly and, for the first time, believed this week might actually be a good one.

After Gene left, Alan sent separate emails to Bill and Larry. Both men responded within an hour to Alan's invitation to have lunch. The plan was falling into place.

PART IV

I firmly believe that any man's finest hour, the greatest fulfillment of all that he holds dear, is that moment when he has worked his heart out in a good cause and lies exhausted on the field of battle - victorious.

— *Vince Lombardi*

July 25, 11:35 a.m., Spoons Cafe, McKinney, Texas

Alan arrived extra early knowing that Bill is always early, and he wanted to make sure he got a good table in a corner with his seat facing the door. This would minimize the distractions for Bill and hopefully direct his louder-than-necessary voice to only Alan. He ordered an iced tea and reviewed his notes while waiting for his board chair to arrive.

A few minutes later, Alan heard Bill's voice before he spotted him. Bill has been in McKinney many years and does the small business accounting for half the merchants downtown, including Spoons Cafe. "HAPPY TUESDAY. NICE TO SEE YOU," Bill said to the hostess but loud enough for the entire restaurant to hear.

Alan waved at Bill letting him know he already had a table. After a five-minute tour from table to table shaking hands with people he knew, Bill sat down across from Alan. In hindsight, Alan wondered if they should have met somewhere more private.

"Hi, Alan. How are you? Have you solved our financial problems yet?" Bill asked with a smile.

"Well, maybe," replied Alan, looking Bill in the eyes. "That's exactly why I wanted to meet."

"Alright then, I can't wait hear it. I'm all ears."

Alan laughed in his mind at Bill's word selection. Bill is actually a very nice and warm person in spite of his prickly outside. Alan knew this and tried not to be intimidated. "Bill, for every day of the past month, I have been working on a solution to our financial problem at LCA. I wanted to meet with you ahead of time so that you can steer the board meeting on Thursday accordingly."

"Okay, well I appreciate that, Alan," basked Bill.

Alan continued, "I believe that we really have two challenges to overcome. The first is how we get through the year ahead without a deficit." Bill nodded in agreement with the first challenge. "The second is how we manage the budget in the future to avoid scrambling to make ends meet." Again, Bill nodded in complete agreement.

Alan began by walking Bill through some modest cuts to the budget and the savings that would come from refinancing the debt. Bill seemed impressed that Alan had done his homework.

"I like it Alan. But by my account, that doesn't begin to cover the $300,000 nut before us," Bill said louder than necessary.

Alan scanned the tables around them to make sure no one was paying attention. "That leaves $200,000 to be exact. But any more budget trimming will require cutting into muscle. Therefore, I want the board's blessing to make up the rest with fundraising." There, it was out on the table. Alan braced himself for Bill's reaction.

Bill stared at Alan for a good 30 seconds before speaking. Finally, he began in his usual gruff tone, "You know how I feel about fundraising, Alan. I'm disappointed that this seems to be our only option. For years we have managed to operate within our tuition income." Bill's voice got louder. "We started LCA with a commitment to maintain financial responsibility. Are you telling me that we may have to go back to our families and say otherwise? Back on our word? I still think we have a spending problem, not a fundraising problem."

A couple of diners at nearby tables were now glancing their way, noticing the unhappy words coming from Bill. The waitress even did an about-face sensing it was not the right time to greet the two men. Alan was feeling anxious and defensive. He could tell that his heart was beating rapidly. Bill was being a bully, and he needed to respond.

Alan counted to 10 before speaking. He knew there was going to be a collision between he and Bill and more sparks would fly. He looked back up at Bill and calmly responded, "I appreciate your thoughts, Bill, and have always been grateful for your leadership. But this time I think you are wrong. I manage a tight ship at LCA and have been completely transparent with you and the board from the beginning. We are not going to resolve our differences here at this table. My one request of you today is that we dedicate Thursday's board meeting to this topic. I would like to propose a solution to the board and tap into the collective wisdom around the table. Can you do that for me?" Alan finished and was prepared to get up and leave if Bill's anger continued to escalate.

Then something incredible happened. Bill stared at Alan a half a minute or so and actually calmed down. "Alan, I can see you are convicted on this issue. I think your request is a reasonable one. Yes, you have my commitment that the board will give you our undivided attention and open-mindedness to your ideas."

In Alan's mind, his jaw dropped in disbelief. He had watched Bill run roughshod over other board members so many times before, but no one ever stood up to him. He held Bill's gaze and nodded. "Thank you, Bill. You have my word: I will not waste the board's time."

The waitress now approached, sensing a lull in the altercation. "Everything all right here?" she asked while half smiling. "If I need to get the bouncer over here, just say the word."

Bill laughed out loud and soon Alan joined in. The waitress set down glasses of water and put menus in their hands, promising to return for their order in a few minutes.

Alan decided to make a confession. "Bill, I asked for this meeting so that I could hear your reaction outside of the boardroom. I wanted to avoid the argument in front of the other board members. You have made known your position on fundraising in the past, and I knew you would be disappointed with the direction I am proposing. But sometimes your reaction in the board meetings shuts down all productive discussion." Alan kept eye contact through his speech. "What I am looking for on Thursday, Bill, is the board's blessing to proceed."

"I know I can come off a bit grumpy, Alan. My wife and kids tell me that all the time. But my real fear at LCA is that we end up spoiling the culture we have created by having nickel-and-dime fundraisers like spaghetti suppers, auctions, and cookie dough sales." To Alan's surprise, Bill was actually speaking at a reasonable decibel level.

Bill continued, "I should probably come clean, Alan. I met with Father Frank, the president of St. Francis Catholic School in Plano, a couple of months ago. He shared with me that they reached a similar financial dilemma a few years prior and needed to start fundraising. They hired some development staff and immediately started doing events, including a golf tournament, a gala, and fish fries during lent. But the kicker was that they really weren't making money for the school. They were actually spending most of the proceeds covering their fundraising staff and event costs. It's a circus."

Over lunch, Alan listened to Bill share his heartfelt concerns about fundraising and, for the first time, began to understand him. Bill loved LCA, and his motives were pure. Alan's confidence was growing, and he was beginning to believe that Bill, the board member he had feared most, might just end up being an advocate for the plan he would propose Thursday night.

That evening when Alan got home, he debriefed with Carol. "Who would have thought that Bill's concerns for fundraising at LCA were so deep and heartfelt?" observed Carol. "Maybe he's a big teddy bear on the inside."

July 26, 11:45 a.m., MinTec

Alan approached the reception desk on the 7th floor of the MinTec building with sandwiches from Subway in hand. Alan decided last evening that Larry Dolan's office might be a bit more discreet and a better location for their lunch meeting. He texted Larry and offered to bring lunch so they could talk in private. "Hello, I'm Alan Morgan, here to see Larry Dolan."

Larry started his career in public accounting working for one of the big auditing firms. While he did not choose it, Larry ended up leading audits for companies in the tech industry. One thing led to another and eventually he was recruited by a client that led to his current role as the CEO of a tech company serving Texas and Oklahoma.

A couple of minutes later, Larry appeared and invited Alan back to his office. Palatial in size and decor, Larry's office reminded Alan that there is big money in technology. "Wow, what a beautiful place to work, Larry."

"It's a bit over the top, I know. I am told this is what I'm expected to have in my role. I actually do most of my work in that small office over there." Larry pointed to a door in the corner that led to a normal-sized office with a desk that looked like where someone who worked for a living sat.

Larry led Alan over to a sitting area that included two large leather sofas and a couple of matching chairs. "Make yourself comfortable. I'll get us some bottles of water to go with the sandwiches."

Alan and Larry caught up on personal matters while eating their lunch. Larry and his family had just returned from a vacation to the Cayman Islands, where the entire family went scuba diving. As Larry was sharing the highlights, Alan noticed that the walls of Larry's office were adorned with underwater photographs, many of which included scuba divers—probably Larry and his family.

As Alan was gathering up the sandwich wrappers to throw away, Larry asked, "What's on your mind today, Alan? I can only imagine that it has something to do with the board meeting tomorrow night."

"Well, yes, it does, actually. Before I dive into that, can I ask you a question, Larry?"

"Of course."

"In your business, how do you divide your time between the quality-of-service side and the sales-and-revenue side?" inquired Alan.

"That is a very insightful question, Alan. I wrestle with balance of those two elements every day. I would have to say that the technology service side is more intuitive for me because that is what truly makes our company unique. But I also have to keep focused on new business development all the time. A great service means little if we can't get it to market. The short answer is, my board makes sure I stay focused on both."

Alan nodded in understanding, grateful that Larry was willing to answer his question. "You know, to a degree, I wrestle with the same balance of issues, albeit on a microcosm of the scale you wrestle with every day. I want to be certain LCA is providing the very best Christ-centered education possible, but I also need to ensure there is adequate revenue to pay the bills."

Larry jumped in, "I guess you're right. I know the financial issues have been a heavier weight on you lately. How is the balance?" asked Larry with a compassionate tone in his voice.

Alan chuckled, "About 80/20 right now, given the subject matter of the last board meeting."

"What are you thinking, Alan? Have you come up with any ideas?"

"As a matter of fact, yes, I have. And that is the very reason I wanted to meet with you today," Alan began. "I have done what the board asked and looked for all possible cost savings. I am still about

$200,000 out of balance. And I have concluded that I can make that up with fundraising."

Larry nodded in understanding and then calmly delivered a lecture to Alan that he did not see coming. "Okay. That is your prerogative as the head of school to solve the problem. I'm not one to candy coat the job and responsibility you have, Alan. You are the CEO, and these are your decisions to make, not the board's. We pay you to run the business. It's our job as the board to support you in your decisions while protecting the vision, mission, and integrity of the school. And if you can't run the business, then it's our job to find someone who can."

Alan sat wide-eyed at what he just heard from Larry. In plain words he said, *Fix it or you're fired*. Alan replied, "I do understand my responsibility, Larry, and I fully accept the consequences of my decisions. But I'm not sure the rest of the board agrees that these are my decisions. I feel handcuffed at times, especially when it comes to fundraising."

Larry conceded that point. "I agree there are some around the board table who seem less open to that path."

Larry listened intently for the next 40 minutes as Alan walked him through his proposal and the logic of his argument for fundraising. He talked about the tuition threshold and the law of diminishing returns. He offered statistics to support why fundraising is necessary in most private schools. And he finished with an explanation of the two sets of customers that LCA has and the need for all LCA leadership to embrace them both.

When he finished, Larry smiled and said, "That was beautiful, Alan. And that is why you are the right person to be head of school at LCA."

"Thank you, Larry. That means a lot coming from you. But what I really want is your support in the boardroom tomorrow. There will be objections, and I will gladly take them on one by one. But it would be nice to know you are in my corner."

Larry then offered, "I know there are some voices on the board that tend to drown out others. I can help you with that, but you need to make the compelling case on your own."

Alan agreed and thanked Larry for his time. As they were walking back toward the reception desk, Alan stopped and asked Larry, "Do you ever use outside consultants to help your company?"

"All the time—to help us market and promote the business, to help us organize for growth, to help us develop better systems and processes."

Alan asked one more, "Why do you need to go outside for that guidance? Why not hire staff with that expertise or rely on existing staff?"

"For many reasons, but mostly because we are too close to the challenges that hold us back. We need someone who has perspective and can push us to do things we would likely not do on our own. I learned long ago that the only way you can truly experience growth is by being willing to break some things that need to be rebuilt in a different way. The breaking process can be painful, but that is the only way to growth," Larry added.

As Alan left Larry's office, he couldn't help but see the similarity in Larry's last message to what Gene had told him a few weeks ago.

July 27, 5:59 p.m., Lakeview Christian Academy Boardroom

"Can I get a motion to call this meeting to order?" asked Bill. The board members worked through their normal Robert's Rules of Order routine to start the meeting and approve the minutes from the last meeting. After a few brief reports from the various standing committees, Bill announced to the board that Alan had requested most of the time this evening to propose a solution to LCA's financial crisis.

"Alan, the floor is yours," said Bill as he moved to another seat around the table to better see Alan speak from the head.

To say that Alan was nervous would be a gross understatement. He knew the significance of this meeting and that he would likely face some conflict. But he had been through it many times in his head, twice in front of the mirror, and once in front of Carol. He was ready.

Alan began, "Thank you, Bill. And thanks to all of you for giving me the time tonight to walk through a plan that I personally believe will not only solve LCA's challenges in the coming year, but for years to come. I want you to know that I have taken the charge you gave me very seriously and have spent nearly every waking moment these past few weeks thinking and praying about how to fix our money problems."

Alan took a moment to scan the faces around the table. There was Bill who always looked mad; Stan who was constantly looking at his phone; Jane, the youngest by a decade and always enthusiastic; Mary who always backed Bill; Catherine, the board's prayer warrior; Mike, master of conflict avoidance; and Larry, successful businessman and always impeccably dressed.

All were looking attentively at Alan except Stan, who was sneaking a peek at his phone. Alan continued, "I want to pick up exactly where we left off at our last meeting and address each of the options that we collectively brainstormed to address our projected financial shortfall."

Alan displayed a PowerPoint slide on the screen behind him. "Let's walk through the potential cost savings first. There are some savings to be had by refinancing our debt. I have already begun that process and that, along with some additional budget cuts, will reduce our projected $300,000 deficit this year by $100,000." Alan saw smiles and nods around the table as he expected from this bit of good news.

"As for laying off faculty and salary cuts to administrators, I do not believe either is a viable option. LCA has been blessed with amazing faculty who choose to teach here for a salary that is already 10 percent less than the public school system pays. Every faculty position is needed to teach the classes we have committed to. And cutting salaries would be a slap in their face and almost certainly lead to loss among our team."

Alan tapped his laptop, causing a red line to appear through that item on the slide.

"Cutting tuition assistance was the next idea. But cutting tuition assistance would only result in further loss of students and revenue because those families are still paying for most of the cost of education. This action would only aggravate our financial problem." Heads nodded in agreement.

He then tapped his computer once and another red line appeared, then two more taps to produce red lines through the next two items. "As for slow paying our vendors and borrowing from next year's tuition payments, I am not comfortable with either of them. From my perspective, any savings realized would not justify the breach in integrity both tactics represent."

That last statement caused a couple of winces among the group, mostly from the two who had originally suggested those ideas. "Let me add that these were both viable ideas worth considering given what LCA is facing, so I am not standing in judgment," Alan added, causing the wincing faces to relax.

There was one remaining item on the cost savings list titled Other Budget Cuts. "The last item is where I believe we could make up the balance if we had to solve this entire problem without working on the revenue side of the equation." Alan braced himself because he knew there would be some fireworks coming.

"Finding $200,000 more in cost savings all boils down to answering one question over and over: *what is core to a Christ-centered education?* I first reviewed our mission statement for guidance. Can anyone around the table recite it from memory?" Alan again glanced around the table for a willing volunteer.

Catherine spoke up. "I can. *Lakeview Christian Academy equips students to embrace biblical truth, strive for academic excellence, and model Christ-like leadership in their homes and communities.*"

Alan added, "That should sound familiar, as many of you helped craft it. I then went through our proposed budget item by item, using our mission statement as a lens, and asking the question: *core or not core?* until I found the cuts." There were now a few smiles around table as a few board members began to think Alan may have solved the financial problem.

"I started with the largest budget items—*our faculty and staff, core or not core?* Core, of course. We cannot fulfill our mission without teachers. *Buildings and grounds maintenance, core or not core?* Core again. We must have and maintain appropriate space in which to carry out our mission." Alan took a deep breath in preparation for the next one. *"Athletics, core or not core?"* Then after a pause, he stated boldly, "Not core."

Every member of the board stirred in their seats, and it was Bill who spoke first. "What did you say? Not core? Our sports teams are an integral part of the school's culture. Are you proposing we discontinue athletics?" As Bill asked the last question, there was noise building as board members were conferring with one another over the blasphemy they had just heard.

Alan spoke loudly to bring order back into the room. "Bill, to your question, I don't know if discontinuing athletics is the right decision. But look at it through the lens of our mission statement and think through the answer to the question yourself. Is having a football team core to fulfilling our mission as a Christian school?"

Bill replied before thinking, "Well that is just BS" (only he said the actual word). The shock of Bill's cursing brought immediate quiet to the room, and he was immediately embarrassed upon realizing he said the word out loud.

Larry was the only board member sitting back in his chair with a half-smile on his face. Larry spoke up during the silence. "I think

Alan has a point here. If he is charged with carrying out our mission statement and must operate within the financial limitations that currently exist, then everything that is not core should be on the chopping block. Alan, please continue."

Larry's comments brought focus and attention back to the matter at hand, and a few heads began to nod, conceding the point. Alan continued walking the board through other budget items that included the arts, field trips, and many other co-curricular and extracurricular activities. "If we cut all of these items, we will balance the budget this year," Alan concluded.

Blank faces stared back at Alan as the reality of his logic set in. Bill was red-faced furious, but still too embarrassed to speak up due to his unintentional flub a few minutes before.

After a moment of silence to allow the weight of the circumstances to be felt, Alan proceeded. "As I stated a moment ago, these drastic cuts would only be necessary if we accept the current revenue projections as unchangeable. But let's revisit the revenue side anyway."

Alan tapped his laptop and the revenue list the board had brainstormed at the last meeting appeared on the screen. The first item on the list was tuition. Alan took a few minutes to explain the law of diminishing returns and cited the past few years' dropping enrollment as evidence. "Any increases beyond inflation will result in enrollment decline and, consequently, a net loss in revenue. And adding additional fees to pay for things that used to be covered by tuition will only be seen by our school families as a tuition increase in disguise." Again, heads nodded.

Alan had crossed off every item on the revenue side except the last one. "That brings us to the final item, the possibility of fundraising to supplement tuition revenue. I know that LCA has been resistant to the notion of doing annual fundraising. Bill, you always say we shouldn't have to do fundraising if we operate the school like a business." Bill's eyes widened at being quoted.

"But did you know," Alan continued, "that nearly all private schools in America require supplemental fundraising to cover annual operating expenses?" Alan displayed a slide showing national statistics. "While very few schools manage without supplemental revenue, over 90 percent of Christian schools receive supplemental support ranging from 5 to 40 percent of their budgets—that support coming from fundraising or subsidies from sponsoring churches."

"While we are a nonprofit business to an extent, we are not a typical business that can charge whatever it needs to for its services or products. We are, on the other hand, a typical Christian school that charges a fair tuition rate for its service and that maximizes the number of children who have the opportunity to experience it."

Alan let that thought hang in the air a minute before proceeding.

"I therefore propose we make a shift in our culture to begin active fundraising to supplement tuition and make it possible for LCA to continue our athletic, arts, and other co- and extracurricular activities."

CHECKMATE was the word that popped into his mind. For a brief moment, he pictured himself as Perry Mason concluding his closing argument.

Bill finally spoke up after a 60-second period of silence during which the board's minds were processing. "Okay, Alan, thank you for the proposal. We'll take it under advisement as we move into executive session to make our decision."

Alan's brief sense of confidence crumbled away as he realized that major conflict was coming. "Bill, before you move into executive session, I would like to respectively challenge the premise of your next steps."

Bill couldn't believe his ears. Suddenly everyone in the room was rapt with attention as they prepared to witness a fight. The air was getting heavy with tension. "What are you talking about, Alan? I just told you what we were going to do."

Now more nervous than ever, Alan proceeded with a quivering voice, "Bill, again, with all due respect, I do not believe it is the role of the board to make this decision. I am the head of school and, as such, serve at the board's pleasure. You pay me to run the school and to make decisions that lead to achieving the goals of our mission. If the board would like to discuss this matter further with me, I will stay here all night to do so. But it is my decision to move forward with a plan for fundraising, not yours. The only decision I will accept coming out of executive session is whether or not you want me to continue as the head of school for LCA."

Tension was now heavy in the room, and some members of the board were wide-eyed in shock over Alan's assertive stance. Alan felt sweat running down his forehead. He realized that he was all in on this matter and that things would never be the same between Bill and him after his speech.

"WELL, THAT'S JUST BULL!" shouted Bill, stopping himself before repeating the earlier error.

Larry chimed in, calm and collected as always. "Bill and fellow board members, Alan is correct. It is not our job to manage Lakeview Christian Academy. We are its governing board responsible for making sure the school adheres to our mission and holding it financially accountable. We have no more business making a decision on specific fundraising plans than we do with deciding who the next math teacher will be. That is why we have a head of school."

Some heads were nodding in agreement as Larry spoke. Both Stan and Mary were watching Bill's face for fear of his reaction. Bill was still red with anger.

Larry continued, "If anyone feels differently, then we should take some time to review our board bylaws. And we should spend some time this evening in executive session to further discuss our role as a board. But I am standing with Alan on the issue at hand. Whether I agree with every aspect of his fundraising plans or whether I might do it differently if it were me are not relevant. As a governing board, we have no business meddling in management decisions."

Larry looked at Bill and spoke in a quieter tone. "I know you care deeply about this school, Bill. Everything you do for LCA comes right from your heart. You are exactly the kind of impassioned leader that LCA needed to grow our mission to this point. But we all must be open to new and creative ideas."

Bill's blood pressure was coming down, and his composure was returning. After a few moments of silence in the room, Bill spoke. "I'd like to apologize to all of you for my outburst and behavior. I do love this school, and that's why I sometimes get emotional. Alan, you are a great head of school, and I can't imagine LCA without you. There is nothing more I need to say tonight in executive session that hasn't already been said."

The meeting ended with all board members agreeing to support Alan's plans. And although it was a victory for Alan, he did not feel victorious. He said good night to each board member as they left. When he got to Bill, it was strained and awkward. Alan knew their relationship was forever changed.

July 28, 6:30 a.m., Alan's kitchen table

Over breakfast Alan texted Gene to set up a time to talk and debrief with him about last evening's board meeting. Gene immediately replied saying their talk would have to wait until the end of the day. Alan accepted Gene's terms and added the meeting to his calendar for 5:30 p.m. He then refilled his coffee cup and headed to work at LCA.

As Alan pulled into the school parking lot, he immediately noticed Bill's car. As he parked and got out, he saw Bill do the same. Alan had a brief moment of panic that Bill was going to beat him up. Bill waved and said he needed a few minutes of Alan's time. Alan unlocked the front doors of the school, and the two men walked toward Alan's office without speaking a word.

As they arrived, Alan broke the silence. "Bill, would you like some coffee? I can make a quick pot."

"No, thank you, Alan. I have been up for hours—most of the night actually—and had too many cups already. Besides, I won't need all that much time."

They both sat down at the small table in the corner of Alan's office, and Bill began to speak. "Alan, I am not happy about how the meeting went last night."

Alan began mentally preparing to defend his actions in case Bill wanted to go there.

Bill continued, "I was wrong. And you were right. I lost it last night and behaved in a way that is inexcusable. When I got home, I spent an hour telling my wife the story. When I finished, she emphatically told me I was wrong. She went on to tell me that I have been a bully to you and the other board members for years and that it was about time someone punched me back."

"I couldn't sleep at all after that eye-opening chat with Eunice. So, I started praying. In fact, I spent hours meditating and seeking guidance. Early this morning, after a few cups of coffee, my head finally cleared, and the right path became obvious. Alan, I am going to resign from the board."

Alan raised his hands in a waving-off motion and started, "Now, Bill..."

Bill interrupted, "Alan, let me finish! I am not walking out because I didn't get my way so I'm taking my ball and going home. And I'm not resigning immediately." Alan put his hands down and listened intently as Bill continued.

"I am resigning because I am no longer an effective leader at LCA. I have been around too long and have occupied a role that, frankly, probably should have been passed to others over the years. I took to heart all that you and Larry said last night and believe I need to make some space for newer and younger leadership."

"Bill, you have been a tireless leader since the beginning," Alan inserted.

"In the early years, I was more effective. But I am just now beginning to see what others have probably known for years. I am stuck in the way we have always done things and never willing to try anything new. And I am a bully. I have been told that since my days in the Army."

Alan smiled and said, "Well, maybe you are a little bit of a bully." Both men laughed.

Bill went on to explain that he would like to announce his resignation at the next board meeting and have it be official at the end of December. He wanted everyone to understand his decision and to know he was not walking out in anger. And he wanted to contribute to creating some new bylaws in his final months that would limit the terms and years of all board members. A few minutes later, Bill stood up and shook Alan's hand. The two men then hugged each other.

Alan felt at peace with Bill's decision but also some anxiety. Although Alan agreed that Bill was a bully and close-minded, Bill had been like a father to the school and had always been there.

Alan told Gene the entire story later that day. Gene listened without interrupting for 45 minutes. Finally, Alan asked, "So what do you think?"

Gene smiled and said, "I think we should get busy raising funds for Lakeview Christian Academy."

Alan tried again. "That's it? No reaction to the sequence of crazy events?"

Gene chuckled this time. "Alan, you handled the meeting last night perfectly. The right things are happening. I know you are still concerned about Bill's hurt feelings, but sometimes that is what it takes to make room for change. The great news is that fundraising will now commence."

Raising to the Challenge

PART V

And those who were seen dancing, were thought to be crazy, by those who could not hear the music.
— Friedrich Nietzsche

July 31, 6:00 a.m., Lakeview Christian Academy

Alan had an unexpectedly restful weekend. He and Carol had a few long talks about the board meeting and Bill's surprise visit the following morning. He woke up early that morning excited about his weekly meeting with Gene.

Gene showed up right on time, and the two men dove right in over their bagels and coffee. Gene led off, "Today we are going to tackle one single prospective donor and plan the experience from start to finish."

Alan took note of Gene's choice of words. "What do you mean by *experience*?"

"A critical factor in relational fundraising is looking at everything we do through the eyes of the prospective donor. Let's take James and Sally Miller for example. How will they experience the way you communicate with, make requests of, and steward them? Our goal is to create an experience for the Millers that is uniquely theirs—one that acknowledges and addresses their passions and interests in LCA, and one that ultimately exceeds their expectations."

"So, you're saying there is more to this than going to visit them with a brochure in hand," Alan offered to affirm his understanding.

"Much more. Let's start with gathering what we know about the Millers. What can you tell me?" asked Gene.

"Well, let's see. They have been an LCA family for about 10 years. All three of their daughters attended LCA. The oldest two graduated and are now in college, and the youngest is still here as an incoming sophomore."

Gene took notes as Alan continued, "All three girls are into the arts, from choir to theater, and they are talented. There is always a Miller girl starring in our productions. In fact, the oldest is studying acting in college and wants to take a run at musical theater."

"Great!" replied Gene. "Have the Millers ever given to LCA?"

Alan sheepishly replied, "We really have never asked them, Gene."

"Okay, I get it. What do Sally and James do for a living?"

"James is an emergency room doctor at McKinney Regional Hospital. Sally works part time in one of those multi-level marketing organizations. I think she sells vitamins or something like that. The Millers do very well."

"Are Sally or James involved or engaged as volunteers with anything at LCA?"

"Yes. Sally is a volunteer with the theater program. She is always around during the rehearsals and performances of our plays helping with transportation and food for the kids involved. And they always host the end-of-year party for the theater kids."

Gene asked, "How much do you budget for your play productions each year? All costs from transportation to the expense of sets and theater rental."

Alan pulled out his copy of the budget and started flipping pages. A few minutes later, after writing a list of numbers and adding them up, he replied, "Looks like $12,750. No wait, really closer to $16,000 all in."

"Perfect!" Gene's voice was picking up excitement. "I think we have enough to create an experience for the Millers."

Gene then put aside his notebook and sat back and crossed his legs. "Alan, let's talk for a few minutes about the philosophy of what we are trying to do."

Alan nodded in agreement, put his papers aside, and looked at Gene.

Gene began again, "You are about to launch a relationship-based fundraising strategy. Tell me what you think that means."

Alan thought for a moment and responded. "I think it means I am going to wine and dine people, so to speak, in the hopes they will write me some big checks. Probably similar to how a salesman might woo a key prospective buyer. Am I close?"

Gene grinned crookedly on purpose and continued. "Not exactly. While there is an element of relationship between you and LCA donors, we want the relationship to be between the donor and LCA's mission. You are simply the ambassador of the mission to the donor."

"How is that different than what I said?" Alan asked.

"Your role as an ambassador of LCA is to help a donor experience the mission of the school in an impactful and personal way. Sales tactics like wining and dining or taking a prospect out for a round of golf rarely fit this strategy. That can feel disingenuous—like you are pretending to be someone's friend so they will give you money."

Alan nodded slowly as Gene's point was becoming clear. "So, it's not really about me, it's about LCA."

"Exactly. Well said," affirmed Gene. "With that mindset, the next step is to craft the prospective donor's story."

"Do you mean that we are actually going to write a story for the Millers?"

"In a manner, yes. But let's stay out of the weeds right now and think of the bigger picture. Do you remember the basic elements of a story? We talked about this a few weeks ago in the context of the broader LCA story."

Alan quickly responded, "Characters, setting, plot, conflict, and resolution."

Gene laughed. "Well, that is what we are going to do, creatively plan and craft a storyboard for how we want each donor to experience the mission of LCA. Let's fill in some of the blanks. Who are the characters?"

Alan was enjoying this process. "The prospective donor and me."

Gene nodded in affirmation. "In the case of the Millers, are there any others? How about the theater teacher?"

Suddenly Alan was worried. "I don't think Mrs. Lipton would be up for asking anyone for money."

"Alan, we are not talking about asking for money yet, and we would not expect Mrs. Lipton to ask the Millers for money. We are talking about characters who can help the Millers experience the mission of LCA in ways that align with their passions and interest."

"I'm sorry, Gene." Alan was embarrassed. "I'm going to shut up for a bit and just listen."

Gene smiled in a way that agreed with Alan's plan. "The point is, we can and should utilize key characters in our story that can add to the quality of the experience. The same is true of the next element—the settings. A common mistake in *a setting* is meeting with a prospective donor in a restaurant. They are often too noisy, and the wait staff, doing their job well, constantly interrupt the flow of conversation."

Alan nodded while Gene continued. "The ideal settings are where the mission happens—here at the school while students are being educated. There is not one parent or grandparent who isn't curious about what their child or grandchild does in the classroom, right?"

Alan jumped in briefly. "I have actually had parents ask me if they could peek through the window of their child's classroom to see how attentive they are."

Gene moved on. "The plot, conflict, and resolution are the actual story. However, the most important of the three is the conflict. Without conflict, any story would be boring. Think about it. Would the story of *Cinderella* really be good if the wicked stepmother and stepsisters were removed? Or would *Star Wars* be any good if you remove Darth Vader and the Dark Side from the story?"

"Of course not." Gene answered his own question and then continued. "The conflict in this application is what we will refer to as the Donor Value Proposition. It is the problem or opportunity that we will present to a prospective donor for him or her to solve. In the case of the Millers, that Donor Value Proposition is LCA's theater productions."

Yet another light bulb suddenly lit up in Alan's head. "I love this. We are literally going to storyboard the manner in which the Millers will experience LCA's theater program and be presented with an opportunity to help fund it."

Gene gave Alan the thumbs up sign. But Alan's smile faded a bit as he thought through the process. He then asked, "Am I really being truthful by making them think the theater program wouldn't happen unless they helped fund it?"

Gene nodded slowly and said, "Do you remember the little exercise we did the other day with your budget and red pen? If memory serves, both arts and athletics would have to be on the chopping block if there is no funding. But the problem is that you are only looking at the conflict. We are still missing the plot and resolution in our story. The plot is the backstory of why LCA must fundraise to make the financial model work—a similar story that you shared with your board last week."

Alan caught a glimpse of the clock on the wall and realized they had already gone 15 minutes over their scheduled time. Gene realized it at the same time and started stacking his things in preparation to leave. "Here is your homework. Think through the elements of the story for engaging the Millers. Be creative, like you would if you were writing a story. Plan on at least two separate meetings with them and how you would utilize each. We can polish your prospect experience storyboard next week."

Alan's brain was racing with excitement after Gene left. Alan had always thought of fundraising as a necessary evil and burden—something that no one in his right mind would look forward to doing. The concepts and philosophy Gene was teaching him, however, made perfect sense and were turning out to be something that was going to be great fun.

August 7, 6:00 a.m., Lakeview Christian Academy

What a week Alan had. Besides working on the Millers' experience storyboard, other things were beginning to happen at LCA in preparation for the school year ahead. Several faculty members were showing up to ready their classrooms with decor and organization, which meant that Alan had to plan time to catch up from the summer with each teacher.

This was always Alan's favorite time of year at LCA. Everyone is rested and refreshed and excited about what the year will hold. Students would soon fill the halls, each a bit taller and more mature than when they left the previous spring.

Gene uncharacteristically arrived a few minutes after their normal start time. "Hi, Alan. I'm sorry I'm late this morning. I had to run to my office to get something for our meeting."

Alan said with a laugh, "For that I may have to cut your fee in half."

The two men went through the normal paces of bagels and coffee. After catching up on family matters, Gene pulled what appeared to be a children's puzzle out of his briefcase. It was a wooden puzzle with about 20 large pieces. When Alan looked closer, he could see that the picture on the puzzle was, coincidentally, Cinderella—one of the examples Gene used to describe the importance of conflict in a story.

"So, we're going to work a puzzle today, are we?" Alan asked in a lighthearted tone.

"In a manner of speaking, yes," replied Gene in the same playful manner. He continued more seriously. "I want you to think about the work ahead of you as building a puzzle. Only the real picture won't actually be Cinderella."

Gene unwrapped the newly bought puzzle from its cellophane and then dumped out the pieces. He quickly reassembled the 20 pieces upside down in the same rectangular wooden frame. He then produced a thick black marker and wrote across all 20 pieces the words *LCA Margin of Excellence $200,000*.

"This is the puzzle you will build in the coming months. Each piece represents a financial gift from a future donor. When the picture is complete, you will have raised the $200,000 needed to fund the activities that represent the LCA margin of excellence."

Alan was smiling broadly, admiring Gene for his innovative tools to teach a concept. "I love this. So then, each piece represents a gift."

"What you are saying is that I need to find 20 people who will donate $10,000 each, right?" By now Alan could read Gene's face when he was on the right track. He was reading the face Gene makes when he is off track. "Not right. Okay, lay it on me."

"You are correct. Each piece will represent a specific amount of money coming from each donor and the amounts will total $200,000, but the individual amounts will be different."

Gene continued, "This is a planning and monitoring tool. I want you to mount the empty frame on your office wall in a place where you will see it every day. It will be a constant reminder of what you need to do to complete the picture and show how far you have progressed."

"As you receive the corresponding gifts, you will place the piece of the puzzle *Cinderella side up* so that others who visit won't know exactly what the puzzle is about. And the picture of Cinderella that gradually gets built will be a reminder of the storyboarding process and the need to be creative with prospective donor experiences."

Alan asked, "What amounts should we put on each piece, and how do I make sure I get that amount? I mean, it will be a coincidence if a donor decides to give the exact amount on the puzzle piece." Alan was trying hard to understand how this would work.

"We are going to use the amounts you determined a couple of weeks ago when you built a financial model. Remember? We will then write the amounts on each puzzle piece. Can you grab the copy of the budget with the red circles and that financial model worksheet you completed?"

Alan handed Gene the marked-up budget and worksheet. Gene continued, "There is an art to this process, and we may have to redo it a few times before we get it right. What we are looking for are budgeted programs that cost the school specific chunks of money. For instance, we know from our discussion last week that theater productions represent about $16,000 in unfunded programs."

Gene pulled a small stack of papers from his case that had a grid of squares printed on them in the same configuration as the pieces of the puzzle fit together. He handed one sheet to Alan and asked him to write in the first box, *Theater Productions, $16,000, Millers*.

He then asked Alan to put in the next box, *Football, $25,000*. The process continued until all 20 boxes were filled.

Gene then looked up at Alan and said, "Okay, we have changed the financial model a bit to match actual projects in the budget. Add up all of the amounts and tell me where we are."

Alan pulled a calculator from his desk drawer and went to work. "Well, $188,500 is what I get. That's pretty close."

"That's great, we are close," Gene added. "Let's go back to the numbers and round them off. Every number should round to a thousand, meaning we should have three zeros after each number."

When that task was completed, the numbers totaled to $202,000. Alan then re-asked a previous question: "So how do we really know how much a donor will give? I mean, the prospects are not coincidentally going to write checks for these amounts."

"We are going to ask prospects to give those specific amounts." Gene said this in a matter-of-fact manner and then watched Alan's facial expression change. Gene also could now read Alan's expressions as well.

Gene jumped in quick by saying, "We need to ask for specific amounts because we need specific amounts."

"But I'm just not comfortable telling someone how much they should give. It feels very awkward, like I'm asking them to measure up to my assessment of them," confessed Alan.

Gene sat back again and prepared to give a lecture. "I understand your concern. Let me come at this from a different perspective that might help address this concern. What if your goal was to get donated the specific textbooks necessary to educate your students? You would need books in all subjects like math, English, history, and so on. Where would you go to get those books donated? More than likely the publishing house that makes them. Would you approach the publishing house and simply ask them to give? If you did, it would be an accident if they gave you what you needed. You would most likely end up with books that do not address your specific needs."

"So instead," Gene continued, "you would share with the publishing house your need for a certain number of books in a specific subject. And they might respond by offering to give you some of what you need, but at least they now have a reasonable basis on which to respond. Asking for money is no different. You need specific amounts to fund specific programs. That is the basis on which your prospects will respond. And if they can't fund the entire cost of a program, they may say they can only fund part of it. But at least they have a rationale for the amount you requested."

Alan did the old mind exploding thing again with his hands. "Is there anything you don't have an answer for? That makes sense. Okay, let's get busy."

They completed the planning tasks by writing the amounts on the back of the puzzle pieces. Gene then explained that the pieces should be stored in his desk drawer and that he could only place a piece if and when the corresponding financial gift was received.

As the final task, Gene helped Alan polish up the storyboard for the Millers. Gene then assigned homework. "Alan, this is a great storyboard of a prospective donor experience. It's time for you to implement the story. Take the initial steps this week, and we will debrief next week."

October 26, 5:30 p.m., Lakeview Christian Academy Boardroom

Alan arrived back at the school and headed right for the boardroom to get ready for the meeting. He was excited because the meeting would be dedicated to two big items. First, Bill would be addressing the board and giving an update on his work with Larry, Stan, and Mary on new bylaws. He would also be announcing the turning over of the gavel to Larry as the new board chair. The second topic would be Alan's update on his fundraising activities, including a testimonial from Sally and James Miller.

Now that school was back in session, Alan wore a tie to the meeting. He decided to add a jacket to underscore the relative importance of the meeting. He wanted to tidy up the boardroom, lay out agendas, get the refreshments set out, and make sure everything was perfect.

At 5:45 p.m., Bill walked in the door. "Hi, Alan!" he said a little too loudly. "I hope I'm not interrupting anything. I just wanted to get here early given this is my last meeting as chair. I'm feeling a bit sentimental about it."

Alan walked over to greet Bill with a warm handshake. "I'm glad you are here, Bill. I understand how you feel. We all feel the same, you know."

"Say, how is your fundraising plan going?" asked Bill.

"Well, you will hear all about it later tonight. But to answer your question—very well. We can see our way to where we need to be." Alan looked at Bill with compassion, not wanting in any way to be sending a told-you-so message.

"I'm pleased, Alan. Thank you for what you did and have been doing. While my departure is bittersweet, I leave with a secure feeling that you are in charge. By the way, this may surprise you, but when are you going to come and ask me to give?"

Alan's jaw probably dropped based on his level of shock. "Uh, I don't know, Bill. Are you willing to consider it?" Alan's voice ended on a shaky note, clearly taken aback by Bill's question.

"I am. In fact, I would be offended if you didn't give me the opportunity to personally support LCA. I love this place. Will you do me the honor of inviting me to give in the near future?"

Alan walked around the table to Bill and looked him in the eye. "It would be my honor. Thank you, Bill." And then Alan embraced him.

Just then Larry walked into the boardroom. "Whoa, what's going on here?" All three men laughed and the moment was over.

The Millers arrived next, excited to be included in the board meeting. Before long, the entire board was there and multiple conversations were happening.

Bill, of course, called the meeting to order at 6:00 p.m. on the nose. After the normal pleasantries and approval of minutes, Bill explained that the balance of time would be given to two key topics, the first of which he would address.

"As you all know, this is my final board meeting as your chair. At the next board meeting in December, Larry will take over, and for the first time in 15 years since the founding of the school, LCA will have a new chair. I want you all to know how much I love this school and treasure the time I have spent working beside each of you over the years. Lakeview Christian Academy will always be part of my life, and I will always be praying for its prosperity and success." Bill's eyes were red and watery.

"Okay, I'm done with the mushy stuff, on to the business at hand," Bill said in his normal boisterous and loud voice. "LCA has grown into a first-class school that requires new leadership at the board level. That is precisely why I am resigning and why Stan, Larry, Mary, and I have reworked our bylaws. We have been a mom-and-pop operation for too long. We need to establish a more professional board that can take our school to the next level."

Bill put his hands up, "Now I am not implying that you all are *not* professional. Quite the contrary. But our policies and bylaws need to ensure that someone like me can't sit in the chairman's seat for 15 years and hold the school back."

Bill proceeded to walk the board through the new terms of serving on the board. There were a few questions, but the board was in agreement that this was the right action to take. The board voted unanimously to approve the new bylaws.

As Bill wrapped up his comments and sat down, Larry stood up to speak. "Bill, you have been LCA's best friend and supporter for 15 years. So, we are none too anxious to let you go now. I'd like to make a motion that we award Bill lifetime honorary board status."

All board members stood and said, "SECOND!" in unison.

"All in favor?"

"AYE!"

This all happened before Bill could object. Larry continued, "Bill, you are no longer required to attend board meetings, but you are always welcome."

Bill was too emotional to speak and was visibly weeping, so Larry suggested a short break before the Millers came in to join the meeting.

Ten minutes later, the board was re-seated and Sally and James Miller stood together at the head. James began, "Good evening. Sally and I are grateful for the opportunity to be before you briefly tonight. We have known most of you for years, and I think you know how we feel about Lakeview Christian."

James looked at Sally, and she picked up the speaking. "All three of our girls have been at Lakeview Christian since we moved to McKinney 10 years ago. Elaine and Rebecca graduated from here, and Lindsay, our youngest, is a sophomore this year. The first thing we want you to know is how grateful and fortunate we are that our girls could be educated at Lakeview Christian. They have been so well prepared for life beyond high school, and for that we thank God first, but then Alan for his amazing leadership and creating the awesome environment here for our kids."

Sally turned back to James, and he began again. "Several weeks ago, near the beginning of the school year, Alan reached out and asked if he could come by the house and meet with us. Our knee-jerk reaction was concern that there was a problem with Lindsay. Alan assured us that all was fine and that he wanted to share some updates about LCA. We set a date later that week."

"When we met that evening, Alan filled us in on all that LCA is doing this year as well as the growth path LCA has been on since the school began. He showed us a couple of charts that illustrated tuition growth over the years as well as the cost of educating a child. We had no idea the actual cost of education had risen so much over the years, and we were shocked to learn that tuition didn't actually cover all of the cost."

Sally took over again. "Alan explained to us the importance of keeping tuition affordable for all LCA families. And we know several families who struggle to keep their kids at Lakeview Christian, so this all made sense to us. Alan then explained that he was beginning an annual funding initiative that would seek additional support from families who are moved to give."

James tagged in. "We assumed Alan's next line was going to be, *Would you give?* Instead he did something unexpected. He said his purpose that night was not to ask us to give, but rather to ask our permission to ask in the weeks ahead. Now Sally and I both went to private schools growing up, so this concept of fundraising was familiar to us. Of course, we were ready to help. But instead, Alan reiterated that he did not want us to give that night. He asked us to be patient and wait for him to better understand the school's specific needs. He then thanked us for our time and understanding and promised to be back in touch with us in the next week."

Several of the board members' faces looked confused as they silently wondered why Alan wouldn't have accepted their giving right then.

"The story gets better," continued James. "About a week later, Alan invited us to come to the school. We thought it was a little odd that he asked us to come at a specific time of day—10:50 a.m. It worked out though because I was on the evening shifts at the hospital that week."

"When we arrived, Alan met us and ushered us right into the black box theater where we took a seat. A student brought us each a bottle of water and then Mrs. Lipton, the drama teacher, introduced us to her class."

Sally cut in. "Of course, we already knew most of the kids. Our daughter Lindsay is one of them."

James continued, "We knew that they had been working on a new production since mid-August because Lindsay was spending lots of time up here weeks before school began. Mrs. Lipton informed us that we were about to witness the dress rehearsal of the performance. Of course, it was great."

The Millers were enjoying themselves recounting their story. It was obvious they had probably told it a few times to friends before this evening.

Sally gave James a break. "After the performance, we had the opportunity to visit with the cast members for a few minutes before they dispersed to their next classes. Mrs. Lipton then brought a table and four chairs and placed them right in the center of the black box theater. The table was set beautifully, like it was part of a set. And then Alan came walking back in with lunch for us."

"So, we all sat down together at this beautiful table with candles lit and the theater lights dimmed, and we ate lunch right there in the middle of the theater." Sally suddenly pulled out her iPad and passed around a picture of the table. "Over lunch, Mrs. Lipton shared with us the theater production plans for the rest of the year."

James chimed in, "Then Alan kept his word and finally asked us to give. He explained to us that the theater production budget for the year was about $16,000. He said he honestly had no idea what we were capable of giving or what we might be willing to give, but that he needed to find funding for the theater needs. He then asked us if we would prayerfully consider funding that need. He added that he didn't want us to answer him that day and that he truthfully wanted us to think and pray."

James let that point set in a moment then continued. "Sixteen thousand was honestly more than we were thinking we would give.

Alan gave us a letter that restated his request and a summary of the theater plans and budget."

James looked back at Sally and then to Alan with a smile. "A few days later, Sally and I called Alan to let him know we would be giving the amount he requested."

The board suddenly began to applaud, but James quickly waved his hands to stop it. "Please, please. We are not here tonight to receive praise or to be recognized for our decision. We are here to express our gratitude for this school and the countless ways it has touched our family's lives. And we wanted to share with you the incredible experience that Alan created for us. It was fun, but more importantly, it allowed us to engage with LCA in a personal way."

After the board meeting ended, everyone stayed and visited for another 45 minutes. The board was all smiles.

December 18, 6:00 a.m., Lakeview Christian Academy

Alan greeted Gene with a handshake and a hug. "Merry Christmas, Gene!"

"Merry Christmas to you, too. Did the kids make it home safely?" asked Gene.

"Yes, all the chicks are back in the nest for the next week and a half. Carol is in heaven getting to cook and take care of her babies again." They both chuckled.

The two friends sat down in their usual seats and started preparing their usual Monday morning bagels and coffee. Gene was the next to speak. "Ya know, it has been an incredible six months since we met on the mountain in Red River. You and Carol have become such good friends of ours. That day, we had no idea what lay ahead."

Alan nodded and smiled. "I think back to that fateful day often. Gene, I can't thank you enough for your friendship and for all you have done to help me here at LCA."

Gene looked over at the framed photograph of the mountain in Red River across from Alan's desk. And then his eyes moved just below the photograph to the puzzle of Cinderella. "Only one piece remaining I see. Which one is it?"

Alan hopped up and went to his desk to pull out the last piece. "Let's see, it looks like it is for $3,000 for chemistry supplies. I have a couple of people in mind for this one."

"Let me make this easy for you. The Bensons would like to make a gift to LCA. Count us in for the last piece of the puzzle."

Alan was stunned. "Gene, I can't accept that. You have done so much more for LCA than all of the gifts we have received combined."

"Nonsense. We are giving because we believe in the mission. As I have grown closer to LCA these past few months, I have seen the impact you make. We are excited to support it. And besides, you and Carol are donors to Collin County Family Services."

"We are! And we believe in your mission as well. Thank you, Gene."

Gene and Alan talked through several updates for future fundraising activities in the spring and beyond, including hiring a development director in the coming months. Gene provided Alan with a job description and profile for the kind of person he should seek out.

And then Gene said something Alan wasn't expecting. "I want you to consider engaging a real consultant to help you going forward. I think you will gain much more from a professional who is not your best friend."

Alan suddenly felt like Gene was saying goodbye. "I can't imagine how anyone else could bring the value and wisdom that you do, Gene."

"You can't imagine because you haven't experienced it. Trust me when I say that the right consultant can bring far more value than I can. You need a firm with broader experience who can be a voice to your board. I have a couple of great consultants in mind, former colleagues who I want you to meet."

Alan was pondering his announcement when Gene added, "I'm not suggesting our friendship is over. What I am suggesting is that we just focus on being friends."

Alan felt some relief. "I understand. I will never be able to thank you enough, Gene. You went way beyond my expectations. Just out of curiosity, what kinds of things do you think I might need help with from a consultant?"

"Alan, you are just beginning. You and I addressed the short-term strategy, but we have also talked along the way about the importance of the long-term strategy. You need to build a development operation the right way to grow and sustain the giving that we started these past few months. In addition, we have talked many times about the need for a new middle school building and gymnasium. Trust me when I say, you don't want to borrow all that money."

Alan nodded. "Okay, I see your point. But I would like to get a development director hired and some other things done before I think about bringing on a consultant."

"Here is my final lesson for you." Gene sat back in his chair and crossed his legs. "Find the right consultant first. That doesn't mean that you need to spend big money on consulting right now. But a good consultant will become a trusted advisor to you. A consultant can help you find and train the right development director and help you build the development operation in the right manner."

Gene continued, "And if you are contemplating a campaign for the middle school and gym anytime in the next year or two, you want the time leading up to the campaign to be strategically used to prepare LCA for such an endeavor."

"I was just thinking about the battle I would have to fight with my board in order to hire a consultant." Alan confessed. "But I just remembered a conversation I had with my new chair, Larry Dolan. He uses outside consultants in his business for the same reasons you are suggesting. I think he will understand and support this."

Gene smiled. "How about I make a couple of introductions in the coming weeks, and you can at least begin the process of exploring the possibilities."

"Agreed!" replied Alan. He then got up to shake hands and embrace his good friend.

In the weeks following, Alan and Gene continued to meet every Monday morning over coffee and bagels, and instead of working on raising funds, they began a Bible study.

Raising to the Challenge

Raising to the Challenge

Conclusion

I truly hope you enjoyed the story of Gene Benson, Alan Morgan, and Lakeview Christian Academy. Although I chose to write about a private school navigating some common challenges, these same issues plague the broader nonprofit world. And while Alan Morgan is a fictitious character, he is not unlike many nonprofit executive directors with whom I have consulted and befriended over the past four decades.

The underlying theme of this story is that all nonprofit missions, along the journey toward growth and sustainability, experience great challenges. These challenges are normal growing pains that have all been dealt with before. Overcoming these challenges requires administrators and board members alike be open to doing things differently. The path that leads to significant future growth is always different than the path that brought you to this point.

In the story, Lakeview Christian experiences a crisis that leads to a huge shift in culture. In real life, this often takes longer than the six months over which this story took place. Regardless of the length of time that it may take, change will only happen when there is a plan in place, strong leadership to drive that plan, and a few board members who grasp the key concepts and are willing to champion them to other board members.

There are beautiful and quirky personalities in every nonprofit organization. Learning how to work with these personalities is integral to taking on challenges. And every once in a while, when an individual becomes the source of the problem, the best path forward may be without that individual.

To be sure, every nonprofit must tackle the challenge of raising more money. And the answer is always to engage donors more deeply in relationship with the mission. That part of the story, as well as the best practices and tools utilized, is *literally* the solution to most fundraising challenges.

Please stay tuned for future adventures with Alan Morgan and Gene Benson.

Raising to the Challenge

Raising to the Challenge

Key Concepts

1. **Too often, the willingness to open our minds to new ideas and concepts is only born from facing dire financial circumstances.**

   Sadly, by the time some nonprofit leaders seek help, it is often too late to save their organizations from financial demise. Alan Morgan is not unlike many nonprofit executives who carry the responsibility of running a financially healthy organization. And just as Alan describes Lakeview Christian Academy, most organizations are notoriously slow to warm up to new fundraising ideas and strategies. Just as in the for-profit world, growth often depends on the leaders' ability to adapt to necessary change.

2. **Significant and sustainable growth is possible in every nonprofit organization, regardless of the size, history, and circumstances.**

   Annual financial growth of 10-15 percent, similar to that of Collin County Family Services that Alan discovered while researching Gene Benson, is realistic and replicable in most organizations. However, leaders must be open and willing to change their fundraising approach and model. Few donors give to their capacity, and most donors have simply never been engaged in ways that acknowledge their needs and what they may seek through their giving.

3. **All nonprofit organizations desire and require more funding to sustain and grow their missions.**

    There are no exceptions to this statement. Every nonprofit organization in existence desires mission growth—and mission growth always requires more funding. However, significant and sustainable funding growth will not occur from doing the same events and activities (gala, auction, golf outing, appeal letters, etc.) a little bit better. Significant growth can only occur through new ideas and strategies that engage donors more deeply with your mission.

4. **Every nonprofit should have a second mission statement defining its mission to donors.**

    Read nearly every nonprofit organization's mission statement and try to find something that acknowledges the donor. If all nonprofits have two separate, equal, and codependent missions, then they should also have a second mission statement to address the mission to donors. This will help the board own the second mission and provide a lens through which new development initiatives can be viewed and vetted.

5. **Special event fundraising is usually the first and worst idea to grow funding.**

The most common fundraising activities in America are special events. Galas, golf outings, and auctions are a dime-a-dozen, and few are done well. Consequently, this is usually what comes to mind when board members begin to brainstorm ways to grow fundraising. Special events are fine in moderation, but they represent the path of least resistance, are usually the lowest return on investment, and are always the least sustainable source of income.

6. **Every nonprofit has donors who have capacity to give well beyond what most believe is possible. The goal is to engage donors in a transformational experience.**

Engaging donors in creative ways that serve their passions and interests can open doors to new levels of involvement and giving. Unfortunately, most nonprofits miss this point and large donors are often underwhelmed. It is that "underwhelmed feeling" that many define as "donor fatigue." If the goal with donors is to exceed their expectations and send the message that their decision to give is the best one, the sky is the limit.

7. **Crafting the broader story for a nonprofit mission must utilize the margin of excellence—the part of the mission for which you must seek funding—as the story's conflict.**

Every nonprofit organization must have a compelling elevator speech to tell—one that includes the critical elements of a story (plot, conflict, and resolution). The conflict must represent challenges to overcome and/or opportunities to seize that funding can resolve. This is what can be termed as the *margin of excellence* for most nonprofit organizations—the programs and activities that would not be possible without all or a portion of annual funding.

8. **Matching donors' passions and interests to projects within a nonprofit's budget is integral to achieving capacity giving.**

Scaling down the *margin of excellence* to specific projects that individual donors can fund is a strategic means of achieving transformational experiences and, consequently, significant growth in giving. While this strategy temporarily restricts funding, funding is only restricted to things that are absolute expenses for a nonprofit organization.

9. **Building a financial model will help nonprofit leadership strategically understand the specific financial gifts necessary for success.**

A financial model in the form of a block chart can serve as a powerful tool to monitor progress and illustrate to leadership the key *pieces of the puzzle* needed to achieve goal.

In the story, Gene utilizes a 20-piece puzzle for Alan to assemble as each gift is secured.

10. **Anticipating and preparing for resistance to a cultural shift in fundraising will alleviate many concerns.**

    Any time there is a change in the culture of a nonprofit, there will always be some resistance. Anticipating the sources and types of resistance and then creating strategies to address them are key to achieving success. This plays out in the story when Alan meets with two of his board members prior to the board meeting where he anticipated great resistance.

11. **Storyboard a prospective donor's experience with creativity. Ask what wouldn't you do to help a prospective donor truly experience your mission?**

    Take the time to collaborate and brainstorm ideas with colleagues when planning out a donor experience. Approach it as if you are writing the donor's story, anticipating how he/she will react to each part of the experience. Get creative with the ways in which you engage a donor. Try to get beyond the traditional site tours and brochure presentations that tend to be the norm.

www.ingramcontent.com/pod-product-compliance
Lightning Source LLC
Chambersburg PA
CBHW052353220526
45465CB00003BA/1094